VISUAL QUICKSTART GUIDE

MICROSOFT EXPRESSION BLEND 2

FOR WINDOWS

Corey Schuman and Robert Reinhardt

Peachpit Press

Visual QuickStart Guide
Microsoft Expression Blend 2 for Windows
Corey Schuman and Robert Reinhardt

Peachpit Press
1249 Eighth Street
Berkeley, CA 94710
510/524-2178
510/524-2221 (fax)

Find us on the Web at www.peachpit.com.
To report errors, please send a note to errata@peachpit.com.
Peachpit Press is a division of Pearson Education.

Copyright © 2009 by Corey Schuman and Robert Reinhardt

Development Editor: Bob Lindstrom
Project Editor: Nancy Peterson
Production Editor: Myrna Vladic
Copy Editor: Elissa Rabellino
Tech Editor: Marvin Varella
Proofreader: Joanne Gosnell
Compositor: Jerry Ballew
Indexer: Emily Glossbrenner
Cover Design: Peachpit Press

Notice of Rights

Notice of Liability

Trademarks

ISBN-13 978-0-321-41223-2
ISBN-10 0-321-41223-0

9 8 7 6 5 4 3 2 1

Printed and bound in the United States of America

Dedication:

To Mary and Jack, your love means more to me than you'll ever know—*CS*

Special Thanks to:

Robert, it has been an honor and privilege working with you on this book. I would also like to thank Nancy and Bob for your patience and guidance. Thanks to Schematic for the support and encouragement, which made writing this book possible. Thanks to Matt Coble, John Ferguson, and Ryan Taylor for letting us use a couple of your finest pictures.

Finally, thanks to my son Jack who makes every day worth getting up for. And the biggest thanks to my beautiful wife Mary. You have been the backbone of our family while I stay up late writing. I couldn't have done this without you.—*CS*

TABLE OF CONTENTS

TABLE OF CONTENTS

INTRODUCTION

Two years ago, Microsoft started to release community tech previews (CTP) of a product that was codenamed Sparkle. This tool had an impressive mission: to enable Windows developers and, for the first time, Web designers to more easily build powerful desktop applications with rich graphic user interfaces (GUIs). Sparkle evolved into Blend, a part of the Microsoft Expression product family. In this first edition of *Microsoft Expression Blend 2: Visual QuickStart Guide,* you will learn how to use Blend to build Web graphics and user interfaces.

What Is Expression Blend?

Simply put, Expression Blend is a tool that helps you build rich GUIs for desktop or Web browser deployment. Blend has many of the drawing tools that you'd expect in a graphics program, as well as a familiar canvas (called the Artboard), organizational controls, and panels that enable you to control nearly every aspect of your project and all the elements within that project.

Unlike other WYSIWYG editing tools, Expression Blend is based on XAML, a markup language that describes the UI using a human-readable XML syntax. As a result, GUIs created using Blend may be reused by developers to create applications without any conversion into the development environment. In fact, it is even possible to test your application directly within Blend.

What Are WPF and Silverlight?

Blend can create projects using two different technologies: WPF (Windows Presentation Foundation) and Silverlight.

WPF is mainly geared to build Windows desktop applications. It's a native part of Microsoft Vista and can be enabled on Windows XP by updating the .NET framework available through Microsoft Update. Many of the topics covered in this book can be applied to the creation of WPF applications.

Silverlight, on the other hand, is a browser-based technology that requires the addition of a browser plug-in. As of October 2008, Microsoft reported that one in four computers was configured to display Silverlight content.

Silverlight can render rich user interfaces that you've built in Blend, and enable a wide range of runtime asset rendering and playback. You can display popular graphics formats such as JPEG and PNG content within Silverlight, as well as high-quality audio and video files. Silverlight contains only a subset of the features available in WPF, and does not include any native 3D modeling or object-rendering capabilities as does WPF.

When Blend 2 initially was released in early 2008, you could only create content that targeted Silverlight 1.0–capable sites. Silverlight 1.0, though, was entirely based on JavaScript code syntax. Blend 2 was limited as a JavaScript code editor, so it was primarily used for WPF applications.

When Microsoft released Service Pack 1 (SP1) for Blend 2, the update opened a new world of Silverlight power. Blend 2 SP1 supports Silverlight 2 applications! Silverlight 2 is dramatically different from Silverlight 1.0—many of the same controls that you used in WPF applications can now be applied to Silverlight 2 content.

This book is primarily focused on Silverlight 2 projects and its cross-platform prowess. While there's a slowly growing demand for more desktop applications built in WPF, a far greater demand exists for content that can be viewed in a Web browser across multiple platforms. Because Silverlight is available for both Windows and Mac OS X, content created in Blend 2 can be accessed by any Windows or Mac browser with the Silverlight plug-in installed.

When Should You Use Blend, WPF, and Silverlight?

It's difficult to list every situation that may benefit from the use of Blend, WPF, and Silverlight technologies, but to reduce the possibilities, here are a few tried-and-true scenarios:

◆ **Rich user interfaces.** You need to build a user interface for a desktop application or Web site that looks and feels as exciting as the content you've experienced on high-volume Web sites such as NBCOlympics.com's Beijing Olympic games coverage site.

◆ **Media playback.** You need to play audio or video content to create an immersive desktop or Web-site experience.

◆ **Demanding audience.** Your target audience is on the lookout for an engaging experience, which enables them to make full use of their high-powered desktop and laptop computers.

◆ **Rapid prototyping.** Your clients expect quick turnaround time for building and modifying functional Web designs.

What You'll Need

To perform the exercises in this book, you'll need to have:

◆ A Windows XP–based computer with Service Pack 2 (SP2), or a Windows Vista–based computer.

◆ A 1 GHz or faster processor and at least 512 MB of RAM.

◆ Microsoft Expression Blend 2 with Service Pack 1 installed. You can download a free trial of Expression Blend 2 from Microsoft's site at www.microsoft.com/expression/.

◆ An Internet connection to download sample files for this book's exercises.

When Should You Not Use These Technologies?

Unless you need to update a legacy project that wasn't built for WPF, you should probably look into using WPF for new application development that targets Windows XP or Vista.

For Web-based content, plain HTML content is still king. Plug-in–based content, such as that created for Silverlight or Flash, should utilize the features that these technologies serve best. Don't use Silverlight for a text-heavy Web site unless you're adding a special navigation feature for that text that is best served by Silverlight. Plain HTML is still best suited for most of the content you need to find on the Web—and the operative word is *find*. Even though Silverlight was designed with search features in mind, dynamic content is still not easily indexed. Therefore a search engine, such as Google, won't efficiently find content buried in a Silverlight 2 application.

How to Use This Book

This Visual QuickStart Guide has been written and organized for the beginner or intermediate user of Blend 2. If you've just downloaded and installed Blend 2 and want the quickest way to learn the fundamentals of the tool, this book is for you.

The book is divided into three parts:

◆ Chapters 1 through 5 introduce you to the basic tools and concepts that you'll need to start building Blend projects.

◆ Chapters 6 through 9 show you how to enhance your layouts and interactivity using animations, audio/video elements, and triggers.

◆ Chapters 10 through 12 offer you step-by-step instructions on how to build common Blend 2 projects such as a banner ad, a video player, and a desktop image browser.

Feedback and Support

Our most valuable resource for improving this book is our readers. While we've spent many days, weeks, and months researching and applying Blend to real-world projects, we've also had to make choices about which concepts and topics to cover in this book. Because Blend is a relatively new application with a wide variety of uses, we chose to focus on those applications that most immediately and effectively use Silverlight 2 technology and do not require that you know or use other tools such as Microsoft Visual Studio. Your feedback can help us refine future editions of this guide. Please don't hesitate to e-mail us at info@blendsupport.com with your comments and suggestions. We greatly appreciate your constructive criticism and thoughtful insight.

We've created an independent Blend support site where you can share general Blend information, at www.blendsupport.com. You can download example files and locate other resources specifically related to this book at www.blendsupport.com/blend2vqs.

GETTING STARTED

Microsoft Expression Blend 2 includes several panels and project features that you should understand before you dive into the creation of Blend-based projects. In this chapter, you'll create a project and control the layout of panels. You'll also become familiar with the elements of Blend projects, including project folders and the default files required to produce a Silverlight or WPF (Windows Presentation Foundation) application.

Creating a Project

Microsoft Expression Blend organizes files into a single project folder that enables you to efficiently manage all your working files and references. When you create a project, Blend builds folders for References, Properties, and a default XAML (Extensible Application Markup Language) file. In addition, a code-behind file is created for the default XAML file. The code-behind file executes procedures on the XAML you create and edit in Blend.

What Is a Code-Behind File?

In both Silverlight 2 and WPF, the code for interactive behaviors and server transaction—written in C# (pronounced "C Sharp") or Visual Basic (VB)—is placed in a different file than the presentation code (XAML), known as the code-behind file. Having the code in a separate location rather than inline makes a clean separation between the presentation and the business logic. Traditionally in Microsoft development, interfaces would be designed in a graphics program or in Microsoft Visual Studio. Expression Blend was born with the introduction of XAML as the interface design program for Silverlight and WPF development. It's important to note that Expression Blend's domain is the XAML file, while Microsoft Visual Studio owns the code-behind file.

Figure 1.1 Blend displays the Startup window after loading.

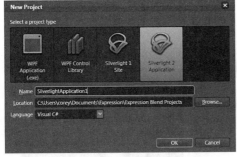

Figure 1.2 The New Project dialog.

To create a new project:

1. The Startup window is the first window that opens after loading Expression Blend. From this window, click New Project (**Figure 1.1**). It is important to note that if you have previously loaded Blend and deselected the "Run at startup" option, you will need to use the next method to open the New Project dialog.

   Or:

   Choose File > New, or press Ctrl Shift N.

   The New Project dialog (**Figure 1.2**) opens. There are four types of projects you can choose: WPF Application, WPF Control Library, Silverlight 1 Site, or Silverlight 2 Application. Examples in this book focus on Silverlight 2 applications.

2. Choose the Silverlight 2 Application.

3. Click OK.

To Open An Existing Project:

1. In the Projects tab of the Startup window, Blend lists the five most recent projects. Select a project. Blend opens the project directly.

   Or:

   Do one of the following:

   ▲ From the Start menu, click the Open Project link.

   ▲ Choose File > Open > Project/Solution.

   The Open Project dialog appears.

2. Navigate to the project file you want to open.

3. Select the file.

4. Click OK.

CREATING A PROJECT

Touring the Workspace

A Blend document consists of the following elements:

Artboard—Displays the graphic content.

Toolbox—Includes all the controls.

Interaction panel—Contains objects and animations.

Project, Properties, Resources panel group—Shows information about files and objects (**Figure 1.3**).

✔ Tip

■ When working with objects in XAML, the visual order is reversed. That is, the farther down an object is in the Objects and Timelines panel or in XAML, the higher the object appears in the visual order.

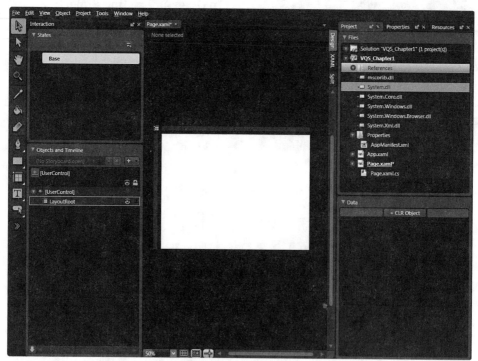

Figure 1.3 After a project is created, this is the default view of Expression Blend.

Figure 1.4 The Properties panel minimizes to these icons when all the panels are hidden.

Working with Panels

Expression Blend allows you to customize your work environment. At times, you will want to create a simpler view of your Artboard by floating or hiding panels.

To float a panel:

◆ Click the ⬛ float button next to the close button to float a panel.

To dock a panel:

◆ In a floating panel, click the ⬛ button to the left of the close button to dock the panel.

To resize floating panels:

◆ In a floating panel, drag the bottom right corner of a panel ⬛ to resize it.

✔ Tip

■ To hide all the panels, press Tab or F4. All panels are hidden except the Properties panel. Instead, the Properties panel minimizes to a group of icons located to the right of the screen. **Figure 1.4** shows the group of icons representing the minimized Properties panel.

WORKING WITH PANELS

About the Project Panel

The Project panel (**Figure 1.5**) contains the files associated with your project. A default project contains a References folder, where the references for the project are located; a Properties folder, where the settings for the project are located; an App.xaml file containing definitions of global application settings/actions; and a default page—named Page.xaml for a Silverlight 2 project or Window1.xaml for a WPF Application. You will notice that App.xaml and the default xaml pages have an expand icon next to them. Clicking the expand icon shows you the code-behind file associated with the xaml page. For more information about the code-behind file, see "What Is a Code-Behind File?" in this chapter.

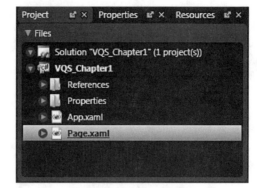

Figure 1.5 The Project panel displays all the files and references in your application.

Working with the Artboard

In the Artboard, you draw and arrange objects. When an object is drawn on the Artboard using the Objects tool in the Toolbox, Blend converts the visuals to XAML. Blend has three main views available in the Artboard: Design, XAML, and Split (**Figure 1.6**).

To zoom in to the Artboard:

◆ *Do one of the following:*

▲ From the Toolbox, choose the magnifying glass. Move the tool over the Artboard and click the area to zoom in.

▲ At the bottom left of the Artboard, choose a preset zoom level (Figure 1.6).

▲ Hold down the Ctrl key while rotating the mouse wheel.

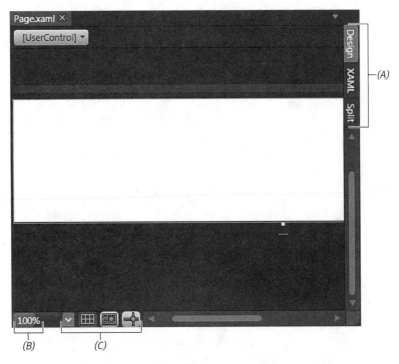

Figure 1.6 The Artboard displays the graphic elements. Toggle between Design, XAML, and Split views (A), Zoom in/out (B), or Show snap grid, Toggle snapping to gridlines, and Toggle snapping to snaplines (C).

To zoom out of the Artboard:

◆ *Do one of the following:*

▲ From the Toolbox, choose the magnifying glass. Move the tool over the Artboard, hold down the [Alt] key, and click the area to zoom out.

▲ At the bottom left of the Artboard, choose a preset zoom level (Figure 1.6).

▲ Hold down the [Ctrl] key while rotating the mouse wheel.

✔ Tip:

■ To quickly return the Artboard to its original size, double-click the magnifying glass in the Toolbox.

To move the Artboard:

◆ In addition to adjusting the horizontal and vertical scroll bars to reposition the Artboard, you can use the Pan tool to move your view in the Artboard. In the Toolbox, choose the Pan tool [🖑]; then drag within the Artboard.

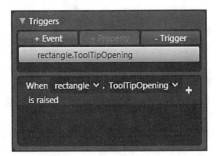

Figure 1.7 The Triggers section allows you to associate actions with storyboards.

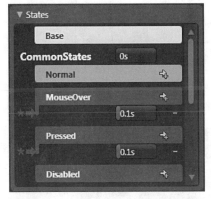

Figure 1.8 The States section defines visual states for Silverlight templates.

Figure 1.9 The Objects and Timeline section shows objects on the Artboard and their hierarchy.

About the Interaction Panel

The Interaction panel has three sections: **Triggers**, **States**, and **Objects and Timeline**. Triggers (**Figure 1.7**) allow you to attach events to storyboards and are specific to WPF applications. States (**Figure 1.8**) permit you to create and manage the visual states of templates and are specific to Silverlight 2 applications. Objects and Timeline (**Figure 1.9**) manage objects on the Artboard and animations.

Visual State Manager

Silverlight 2 introduces a new feature called the Visual State Manager (VSM) that provides an easier and faster way to skin controls. VSM allows you to define states of a control, such as a MouseOver, Pressed, or Checked state. When a control changes states, Silverlight renders the transition between the defined states created by the designer. In Blend, the States panel is used to edit and create states. Only when customizing a control template will you see the States panel with editable content. For more on controls and styling, see Chapter 8, "Styling and Templates."

The Animation Workspace

When you're working with animations, the available horizontal space in the Artboard can become very small and hard to draft out your animations. Expression Blend takes this into account and provides a separate view, called the Animation Workspace. When the Animation Workspace is activated, the Interaction panel becomes horizontal and moves to the bottom (**Figure 1.10**). To activate this view, choose Window > Active Workspace > Animation Workspace, or press F6.

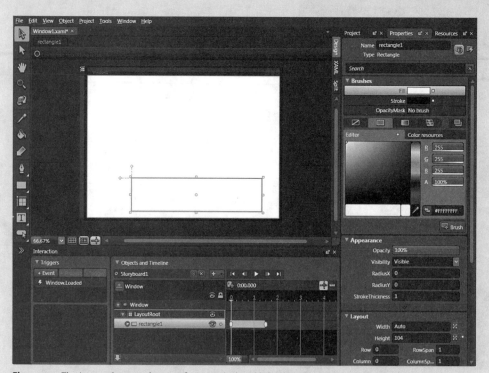

Figure 1.10 The Interaction panel moves from vertical and left aligned to horizontal and aligned to the bottom of the Blend interface.

Figure 1.11 The Properties panel is separated into sections. Each section can be expanded or collapsed by clicking the disclosure triangle.

About the Properties Panel

In the Properties panel, you can apply settings to the objects on the Artboard (**Figure 1.11**). The most prominent section in the Properties panel is the Brushes section. Here you can create solid colors and gradients. You can also use the color swatch and eyedropper to pick colors.

Other Properties panel sections are Appearance, Layout, Common Properties, Transform, and Miscellaneous. These sections are contextual and change depending upon the type of selected object.

CREATING ARTWORK AND TEXT

2

Microsoft Expression Blend is packed with more tools than you'll need for most application development. From basic artwork tools to prebuilt controls such as sliders and tabs, Expression Blend's toolset enables you to quickly craft the nuts and bolts of your layout.

Touring the Tools

The Blend Toolbox is located to the left of the authoring environment. Some 37 tools are available in the Toolbox and its fly-out panels, as shown in **Figure 2.1**. Each tool enables you to add or modify elements in your Blend project.

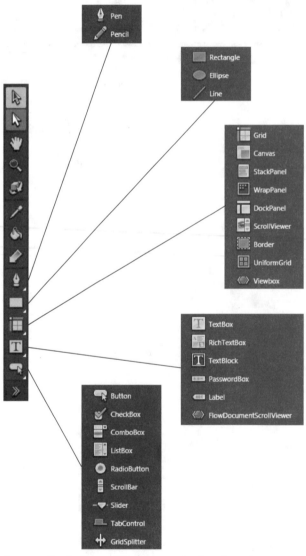

Figure 2.1 The Toolbox and its accompanying fly-out panels.

Table 2.1

Keyboard Shortcuts for Blend Tools	
ICON TOOL	KEY
Selection	V
Direct Selection	A
Pan	H
Zoom	Z
Camera Orbit	O
Eyedropper	I
Paint Bucket	F
Brush Transform	G
Pen	P
Pencil	Y
Rectangle	M
Ellipse	L
Line	\ (backslash)

Selection—Select elements on the Artboard.

Direct Selection—Select individual points within a multi-segment line or shape outline.

Pan—Grab and move the Artboard.

Zoom—Enlarge or shrink the Artboard view.

Camera Orbit—Manipulate the location and view of the 3D camera (for 3D objects only).

Eyedropper—Choose a color within an element on the Artboard.

Paint Bucket—Fill a shape with the selected color on the Artboard.

Brush Transform—Change a fill, stroke, opacity mask, or brush effect applied to an object on the Artboard.

Drawing tools—Choose the Pen or Pencil tool from a fly-out panel. With the Pen tool, you can draw a shape, point by point. The Pencil tool is a freeform drawing tool for the Artboard.

Shape tools—From this fly-out panel, you can choose tools for drawing common geometric shapes and lines on the Artboard.

Containers—Choose a tool to create layout objects on the Artboard from a fly-out panel. The layout objects can contain other elements created with tools in the Toolbox.

Text tools—Choose tools from this fly-out panel to create controls to display text on the Artboard.

Controls—Choose tools to create a wide variety of user interface controls on the Artboard—including buttons and sliders—from this fly-out panel.

Asset Library—Display the Asset Library.

About the Asset Library

If you cannot find an appropriate tool in the Toolbox, check out the Asset Library (**Figure 2.2**). Every control related to your project is located in this panel. Along with the controls, the Asset Library contains styles and media. The most powerful feature of the Asset Library is the speed with which its assets can be searched.

Figure 2.2 The Asset Library.

To search the Asset library for an asset:

1. Click the Asset Library icon in the Toolbox (**Figure 2.3**).

Figure 2.3 The icon in the Toolbox with two right arrows is the Asset Library.

2. You can find assets in the Asset Library in two ways: search via the search text box or browse assets using the tabs.

   Searching displays results as you type the search term. For example, Silverlight and WPF applications have many types of buttons. You can quickly find all buttons by using the search term *Button*. **Figure 2.4** shows the search results for a button in a Silverlight 2 application.

Figure 2.4 Searching the Asset Library for Button displays all available button types.

Figure 2.5 The height and width of the rectangle are displayed as the rectangle is drawn.

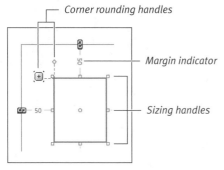

Corner rounding handles

Margin indicator

Sizing handles

Figure 2.6 Selecting a rectangle displays the margins, the corner rounding handles, and the sizing handles.

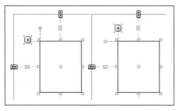

Figure 2.7 Positioning the pointer over the corner rounding indicators changes the pointer to a plus sign.

Figure 2.8 The rectangle on the right shows the result of adding rounded corners to the rectangle on the left.

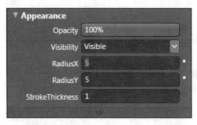

Figure 2.9 Changing the values of RadiusX and RadiusY is a more precise method for modifying the values.

Drawing Geometric Shapes

In the Toolbox, the Shape tools' fly-out panel contains the Rectangle, Ellipse, and Line tools. In this section, you'll use each of these tools to create artwork on the Artboard.

To draw a rectangle:

1. Click the Rectangle icon in the Shape tools fly-out panel, or press M.

2. On the Artboard, drag the rectangle to the desired size (**Figure 2.5**).

3. To draw a square, hold down the Shift key while drawing the rectangle.

To round the corners of a rectangle:

Three types of indicators are attached to a rectangle on the Artboard: margin measurements, corner rounding handles, and sizing handles (**Figure 2.6**).

1. To round the corners of a rectangle, move the pointer to the upper left or right rounding indicators (**Figure 2.7**). Notice the changed cursor.

2. After the pointer has changed to a plus sign, drag to add rounded corners to the rectangle. You can see the results in **Figure 2.8**.

3. Another way to add rounded corners is to modify the values of RadiusX and RadiusY in the Appearance section of the Properties panel (**Figure 2.9**).

✔ Tip

■ Holding down the Shift key while dragging allows you to independently change the RadiusX and RadiusY values.

To draw an ellipse:

1. From the Toolbox, in the Shape tools fly-out panel, choose the Ellipse tool, or press [L]. (Because the Rectangle tool is the default tool in this fly-out panel, click and hold the Rectangle icon to choose the Ellipse tool, as shown in **Figure 2.10**.)

2. On the Artboard, drag the ellipse to the desired size. To draw a perfect circle, hold down the [Shift] key while drawing the ellipse.

To draw lines:

1. From the Toolbox, in the Shape tools fly-out panel, choose the Line tool; or press [\] (backslash).

2. On the Artboard, drag the line to the desired length and angle. As you draw the line, the width and height of the line's boundary area are displayed on the Artboard, as shown in **Figure 2.11**.

Figure 2.10 The fly-out panel for shapes shows the Rectangle, Ellipse, and Line tools.

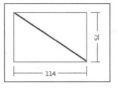

Figure 2.11 A line being drawn on the Artboard. As the rectangle is drawn, the width and height numbers change in real time.

Vector Graphics

When you use the Shape tools in Blend, you're creating a *vector graphic*. A vector graphic is artwork represented by formulas that instruct the rendering platform how lines and fills should be drawn to the screen. Unlike bitmap graphics (such as JPEG or PNG images), vector graphics are not recorded as individual pixels in a grid. As such, vector graphics are much smaller to store in a Blend project. Animated vector graphics, though, can require much more computer processing power than a bitmap graphic.

DRAWING GEOMETRIC SHAPES

Figure 2.12 The Solid Color brush tab is to the right of the No brush tab.

Figure 2.13 The Editor tab.

Figure 2.14 The color channel fields.

Figure 2.15 The Eyedropper tool of the Editor tab.

Creating Solid Color and Gradient Brushes

In Blend, the Brushes section in the Properties panel occupies the majority of interface real estate. Using its tools, you can completely customize the appearance of most elements on the Artboard. The first way to change an object's appearance is by updating the color. Blend includes three types of brushes: a solid color brush, a gradient brush, and a tile brush (available only in WPF applications).

To create a solid color brush:

1. In the Properties panel, open the Brushes section.

2. Click the Solid Color brush tab. (**Figure 2.12**).

3. Click the Editor tab's color grid to choose a color (**Figure 2.13**).

   Or:

   Enter custom values in the R, G, B, and A color channel fields in the Brushes section (**Figure 2.14**).

To select a color using the nested Eyedropper tool:

1. In the Properties panel's Brushes section, go to the Editor tab and click the Eyedropper icon (**Figure 2.15**).

2. Move the Eyedropper tool across the window. As you move the tool over other elements on the window, the color in the Editor tab updates to the color currently located under the tool.

3. Click the desired color to select it.

✔ Tip

- If you want to sample a color displayed on your screen outside of the Blend authoring environment, first make sure Blend is not maximized but still visible, also known as the Restore mode of a window. Then select a color using the Eyedropper tool.

CREATING SOLID COLOR AND GRADIENT BRUSHES

19

To create a gradient:

1. In the Properties panel, open the Brushes section.

2. Click the Gradient brush tab (**Figure 2.16**).

3. The gradient slider appears underneath the color grid (**Figure 2.17**). Black and white are the default colors for the gradient.

4. To add a color to the gradient, click anywhere along the gradient slider. This action adds a new gradient stop selector, which is a color indicator along the gradient slider where there is a color stop (**Figure 2.18**).

5. To change the color of a gradient stop, click the gradient stop arrow, and then choose the desired color from the color selector.

   Or:

   Enter new values in the RGBA fields to the right of the color selector.

6. To remove a gradient stop, drag the gradient stop selector away from the bottom of the gradient slider.

Figure 2.16 The Gradient brush tab.

Figure 2.17 The gradient spectrum in the Editor tab.

Figure 2.18 Clicking along the gradient slider adds a new gradient stop selector.

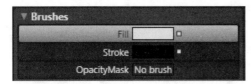

Figure 2.19 Fill is selected by default.

Setting the Fill Attributes

Four fill types are available in Blend: no brush, solid color brush, gradient brush, and tile brush (available only in WPF applications).

To assign a fill:

1. Choose an object on the Artboard or from the Objects and Timeline panel.

2. In the Properties panel, in the Brushes section, click Fill (**Figure 2.19**).

3. Choose a solid color brush or a gradient to apply to the fill. (See the previous section, "Creating Solid Color and Gradient Brushes.")

Setting the Stroke Attributes

Strokes, like fills, can have no brush, a solid color brush, or a gradient brush.

To assign a stroke:

1. Choose an object on the Artboard or from the Objects and Timeline panel.

2. In the Properties panel, in the Brushes section, click Stroke (**Figure 2.20**).

3. Choose either a solid color brush or a gradient to apply to the fill. (See "Creating Solid Color and Gradient Brushes," earlier in this chapter.)

To change the end caps of strokes:

1. In the Artboard, choose a path or an object.

2. In the Properties panel, select Stroke from the Brushes section.

3. Expand the Appearance section of the Properties panel. Notice the two properties: StrokeStartLineCap and StrokeEndLineCap (**Figure 2.21**). Refer to **Figure 2.22** to see the three different cap styles that can be applied to lines.

Figure 2.20 Click the Stroke property to set a new value for the brush.

Figure 2.21 Change the end caps in the Appearance section of the Properties panel.

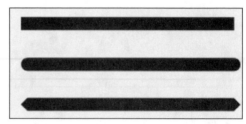

Figure 2.22 The three end cap types available for a stroke are square (top), rounded (middle), and triangle (bottom).

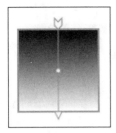

Figure 2.23 The gradient control points.

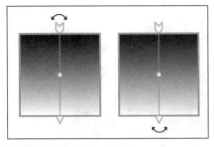

Figure 2.24 The rotate cursor.

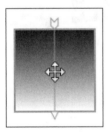

Figure 2.25 The move cursor.

Transforming Gradients

Like solid color brushes, gradients can be applied to fills, strokes, and opacity masks.

To transform a gradient:

By default, the gradient renders from top to bottom. In many cases, you will want to rotate, move, or resize the gradient. The Brush transform tool gives you the ability to manipulate a gradient.

1. From the Toolbox, choose the Brush Transform tool 🖊 .

2. On the Artboard, select an element that has a gradient.

3. An arrow appears over the object to indicate the start and end points of the gradient (**Figure 2.23**). If the arrows don't appear, you will need to add a gradient to the object. See the previous section "Creating Solid Color and Gradient Brushes" for information on how to create a gradient.

4. You can now do one of the following:

    ▲ To change the direction (or rotation) of the gradient, move the pointer directly above or below the arrow. The pointer becomes a curved line, indicating that you can rotate the gradient (**Figure 2.24**). Hold down the (Shift) key while rotating the gradient to snap the rotation in 15-degree increments.

    ▲ To move the gradient, position the pointer over the center dot of the arrow. The pointer becomes a crosshair, indicating that you can move the gradient (**Figure 2.25**). Hold down the (Shift) key while moving the brush transform to constrain the movement along a straight line.

Continues on next page

▲ To resize the gradient, position the pointer over either end of the arrow. The pointer becomes a finger pointer, indicating that you can resize the gradient (**Figure 2.26**). Hold down the [Shift] key while you resize to constrain the transform along a straight line.

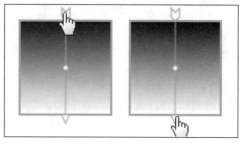

Figure 2.26 The resize cursor.

To create a radial gradient:

1. In the Toolbox, click the Brush Transform tool.

2. On the Artboard, select an element that has a gradient.

3. In the Properties panel's Brushes section, locate the Gradient brush area. In the Editor tab, click the Radial gradient button, highlighted in **Figure 2.27**. The default linear gradient is now a radial gradient.

Radial gradient button

Figure 2.27 The Radial gradient button.

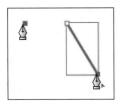

Figure 2.28 Clicking the Artboard with the Pen tool creates a point (left). Click elsewhere on the Artboard to draw a straight line.

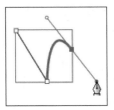

Figure 2.29 Dragging the pointer after creating a new point enables you to draw curves with the Pen tool.

Figure 2.30 Add a node by clicking anywhere along the path. The pointer changes to a Pen cursor with a plus sign.

Figure 2.31 Remove a node from a path by clicking the node.

Figure 2.32 A path drawn with the Pencil tool.

Creating Paths

Using the Pen and Pencil tools, you can create paths in Blend. While the Pencil tool gives you the freedom to draw freehand, the Pen tool is more precise. Curves created with the Pen tool are smoother and lines are straighter, which gives a path a more polished appearance.

To draw a path with the Pen tool:

1. From the Toolbox, choose the Pen tool, or press P.

2. Using the Pen tool, click the Artboard. This creates a start point for your path. To create a straight line, move the pointer to another location on the Artboard and click to create an end point for the line (**Figure 2.28**).

3. To draw a curved line, click and hold down the mouse button at another point on the Artboard. Before you release the mouse button, drag the pointer. This action creates two control points for the curve (**Figure 2.29**).

4. You may now do one of the following:
   ▲ To add a node to the path, move the pointer anywhere along the path. The pointer changes to a Pen cursor with a + (plus sign) (**Figure 2.30**). Click the path to create the point.
   ▲ To remove a node from the path, position the pointer over the node. The pointer changes to a Pen cursor with a – (minus sign) (**Figure 2.31**). Click to remove the node.

To draw a path using the Pencil tool:

1. In the Toolbox, choose the Pencil tool, or press Y.

2. Click the Artboard and draw a path. Compared with the Pen tool, the Pencil tool gives you greater drawing flexibility (**Figure 2.32**).

Touring the Text Controls

Blend has six tools used for text: TextBlock, TextBox, RichTextBox, PasswordBox, Label, and the FlowDocumentScrollViewer. Silverlight 2 applications can utilize only the TextBlock and TextBox controls, while WPF applications can use all six controls.

The TextBlock control is used to display text such as labels on forms, descriptions of elements, or data reported from a database. The TextBox control enables users to input text at runtime.

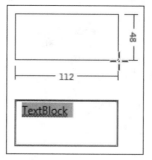

Figure 2.33 Creating a TextBlock control is similar to drawing a Rectangle (top). After creating the TextBlock control, you can edit the text inside (bottom).

✔ Tip

■ Silverlight 1 sites cannot use any Text controls. You must use Silverlight 2 to use controls that are available in the Blend authoring environment.

To create a TextBlock control:

1. From the Toolbox, in the Text fly-out panel, choose the TextBlock tool.

2. Move the mouse pointer to the Artboard and draw a TextBlock area (**Figure 2.33**).

Figure 2.34 In the Properties panel, the Text section specifies formatting for text controls.

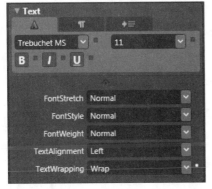

Figure 2.35 The advanced properties for Text.

Formatting Text in the TextBlock Control

The TextBlock control is the most basic text control. Other text controls set their properties in a manner similar to the TextBlock control's.

To set font properties:

1. On the Artboard, select the TextBlock control.

2. In the Properties panel, expand the Text section (**Figure 2.34**). Here you can modify the font family and font size, as well as toggle bold, italics, and underline.

3. You can control even more granular attributes of text formatting within the TextBlock control. To view these properties, at the bottom of the Text section click the down arrow (**Figure 2.35**). In this area, you can change the FontStretch, FontSyle, FontWeight, TextAlignment, and TextWrapping values. Experiment with the values to see their effects on text within the control.

3

MODIFYING GRAPHICS

In the previous chapter, you used a variety of drawing tools in Expression Blend. In this chapter, you will manipulate artwork using the Selection and Direction tools, as well as fine-tune images by making adjustments in the Properties panel.

Using Selection Tools

The two arrows at the top of the Toolbox are the Selection and Direct Selection tools (**Figure 3.1**). The Selection tool is the main tool for selecting, resizing, and positioning an element. The Direct Selection tool can also be used to select and position elements; however, working with paths is the strength of this tool. You can modify the positions of nodes, add curves to paths, and round the corners of nodes.

Figure 3.1 The dark arrow at the top of the Toolbox is the Selection tool, and the white arrow is the Direct Selection tool.

✔ Tips

- The keyboard shortcut for the Selection tool is [V].

- The keyboard shortcut for the Direct Selection tool is [A].

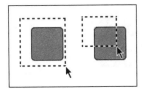

Figure 3.2 Using the Selection tool to draw a rectangle around or on part of an object will select that object.

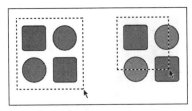

Figure 3.3 These four objects are shown in their selected states. When an object is selected, a rectangle with nodes on the corners and sides surrounds the object.

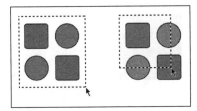

Figure 3.4 Drawing a rectangle either around or on the objects using the Selection tool is an easy way to visually select multiple objects.

Selecting Objects with the Selection Tool

As its name implies, the Selection tool can select any element on the Artboard or the Objects and Timeline panel.

✔ Tip

■ Be sure that the object you want to select is not locked.

To select a single object:

1. To prepare for this task, draw one or more objects on the Artboard.

2. From the Toolbox, choose the Selection tool.

3. To select an object, *do one of the following:*
   ▲ Click an object on the Artboard.
   ▲ Select an item from the Objects and Timeline panel.
   ▲ Drag a rectangle around or on the object on the Artboard. (**Figure 3.2**)

Figure 3.3 shows the objects in their selected states.

To select multiple objects:

1. To prepare for this task, draw multiple objects on the Artboard.

2. From the Toolbox, choose the Selection tool.

3. To select multiple objects, *do one of the following:*
   ▲ Press Shift while clicking objects on the Artboard.
   ▲ Hold down the Ctrl key while selecting items in the Objects and Timeline panel.
   ▲ Drag a rectangle around or on the objects on the Artboard (**Figure 3.4**).

Continues on next page

SELECTING OBJECTS WITH THE SELECTION TOOL

✔ Tip

■ When selecting multiple objects by drawing a rectangle around them, it is not necessary to draw the rectangle around the entire object. As long as the rectangle touches the bounds of the object, it will be selected. This is useful when you want to select from overlapping objects but not select some of those objects.

To deselect an object:

1. From the Toolbox, choose the Selection tool.

2. Hold down the [Ctrl] key while clicking a selected object. This action works for a single object or a group of selected objects (**Figure 3.5**).

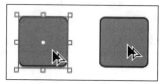

Figure 3.5 Hold down [Ctrl][C] while using the Selection tool to change the cursor to a double arrow. After you click and drag the object, a duplicate object is created and the nodes are hidden.

Cloning an Object

To deselect an object, you hold down the [Ctrl] key and click the object. However, if you drag the object while holding down [Ctrl], you will duplicate, or *clone*, the object. If you're not precise with your sequence of mouse actions, you may be frustrated by the results. In the event this happens to you, you can always press [Ctrl][Z] or select Edit > Undo from the main menu. Despite experiencing this minor frustration, cloning objects on the Artboard can more quickly create interfaces that require multiple copies of the same object. For example, **Figure 3.6** shows the same object cloned.

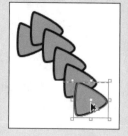

Figure 3.6 Cloning images is a fast and easy way to create multiple objects.

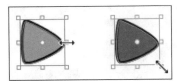

Figure 3.7 Positioning the pointer over a node changes the pointer to a resize arrow. The image on the left shows that you can only change the width, while the image on the right shows that you can resize both the width and height of the object.

Figure 3.8 In the Layout section of the Properties panel, you can manually change the height and width of an object

What Are Transforms?

WPF and Silverlight have the ability to manipulate transforms on any graphic element, including images, video, and text. These are the four types of transforms:

◆ Translate

◆ Rotate

◆ Scale

◆ Skew

In the Transforms section of the Properties panel, you can change the values of these properties. Positioning and sizing elements on the Artboard won't affect the values of the transforms, by default. In contrast, when you create animations (discussed in Chapter 6), the values of the transforms are automatically modified by Expression Blend. (For more information about transforms, see Chapter 4, "Working with Graphic Layouts and Groups.")

Resizing Graphic Elements

There are three ways to resize an object in Expression Blend:

◆ Use the Selection tool to visually resize the object on the Artboard.

◆ Manually change the width and height values.

◆ Change the scale transform values. (Technically, when you modify the scale transform, you are not resizing the object. The object remains at its original size, but appears larger.)

To visually resize an object:

1. Using the Selection tool, select an object on the Artboard.

2. A box appears around the selected object with nodes on its sides and corners. Position the pointer over a node, and the pointer changes to a resize arrow to indicate that you can resize the object (**Figure 3.7**).

3. Finally, drag to resize the object.

To manually resize the width and height:

1. Using the Selection tool, select an object on the Artboard.

2. In the Layout section of the Properties panel, enter new values in the Width and Height fields (**Figure 3.8**).

To resize using the scale transform:

Using the scale transform is trickier than using the previous two methods for resizing. When an object is scaled, the original width and height are not affected. The object is scaled based on the values chosen. Be careful when setting the values of the scale transform because the original aspect ratio is not preserved. To maintain the original aspect ratio, you need to set both the X and Y values to the same number.

1. Using the Selection tool, select an object on the Artboard.

2. In the Transform section of the Properties panel, click the Scale tab. In this tab, you can enter new values for the X and Y scales (**Figure 3.9**). Compare the difference in size, as shown in **Figure 3.10**.

✔ Tip

- When scaling an object, the stroke is also affected. This does not happen when you resize the dimensions of an object.

Figure 3.9 The Scale tab in the Transform section enables you to change the scale of selected objects.

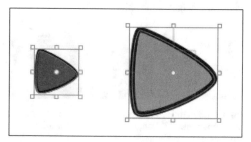

Figure 3.10 Changing the scale of an object does not affect its dimensions, only its visual presentation. On the left is the original object. On the right is the same object scaled to two. Notice that the internal box on the right has the same dimensions as the object on the left.

Figure 3.11 The pointer changes to an arrow with a crosshair when it is placed on a selected object, which indicates that you can reposition the element.

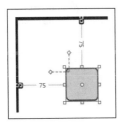

Figure 3.12 Entering Margin values in the Layout section provides precise control over the margins.

Figure 3.13 The Artboard visually shows the margins of objects with set margins.

Positioning Graphic Elements

As you build your user interface in Blend, you will need to move artwork around the Artboard. In this section, you'll use multiple methods to move elements on the Artboard.

To visually position a graphic element:

1. From the Toolbox, choose the Selection tool.

2. Click an object on the Artboard, or on the Objects and Timeline panel.

3. Position the pointer over the object you want to move. The pointer changes to an arrow with a crosshair next to it, indicating that you can drag the object (**Figure 3.11**).

To position a graphic element by changing margin values:

Another way to position graphic elements is by manually setting the margins in the Properties panel.

1. Using the Selection tool, select an object from the Artboard.

2. In the Properties panel, in the Layout section, enter new values in the Margin fields (**Figure 3.12**). The object on the Artboard changes as you modify the Margin values (**Figure 3.13**).

POSITIONING GRAPHIC ELEMENTS

To position using the translate transform:

1. Using the Selection tool, select an object on the Artboard.

2. In the Properties panel, in the Transform section, enter new values for the translate transform (**Figure 3.14**). The object on the Artboard repositions as you modify the X and Y values (**Figure 3.15**).

✔ Tips

- As you move an object with the mouse, a red line appears when the object is next to the edge of the Artboard or another object. This red line indicates a suggested margin for the object.

- You can also use the keyboard to position an element. For greater positioning precision, press the arrow keys to nudge an Artboard object. Hold down the Shift key while pressing an arrow key to nudge in larger increments.

Figure 3.14 The first tab on the Transform panel is the Translate tab. Here you can set the position of the object.

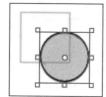

Figure 3.15 Changing the X and Y values of the translate transform repositions the object but retains its original location.

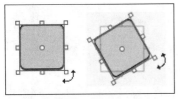

Figure 3.16 Positioning the pointer over a corner node changes the pointer to a curved double arrow.

Figure 3.17 The second tab in the Transform section includes the value for the rotate transform.

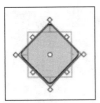

Figure 3.18 Changing the value of the rotate transform updates the object's position on the Artboard.

Flipping, Rotating, and Skewing an Object

Expression Blend offers you several ways to control the appearance of artwork. In this section, you rotate, skew, and flip artwork.

To rotate an object interactively:

1. From the Toolbox, choose the Selection tool.

2. Position the pointer over one of the four corner nodes of an object on the Artboard. The pointer changes to a curved double arrow cursor to indicate that you can rotate the selected object.

3. Drag the object to rotate it (**Figure 3.16**). Hold down the Shift key while rotating to snap the rotation in 15-degree increments.

To rotate an object by a user-defined amount:

1. Using the Selection tool, select an object from the Artboard.

2. In the Properties panel, in the Transform section, click the Rotate tab, and enter a new value for the Rotate transform (**Figure 3.17**). The object on the Artboard rotates as you modify the Angle value (**Figure 3.18**).

To skew an object by a user-defined amount:

1. Using the Selection tool, select an object from the Artboard.

2. In the Properties panel, in the Transform section, click the Skew tab, and enter new X and Y values for the skew transform (**Figure 3.19**). The object on the Artboard skews as you modify the values (**Figure 3.20**).

To flip an object:

1. Using the Selection tool, select an object from the Artboard.

2. In the Properties panel, in the Transform section, select the last tab on the right, Flip (**Figure 3.21**). In this tab, flip the object horizontally by clicking the first button in the tab. The object shown in **Figure 3.22** is flipped on the X-axis. If you want to flip the object vertically, click the second button in the tab.

Figure 3.19 The Skew tab in the Transform section includes the X and Y values for the skew transform.

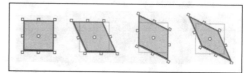

Figure 3.20 The first image shows a rectangle without any skew applied to it. The second image shows an X value of 25 applied to the skew. The third image shows a Y value of 25 applied to the skew. The last image shows X and Y values of 25 applied to the skew.

Figure 3.21 The last tab in the Transform section enables you to flip an object on the X- or Y-axis.

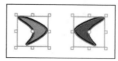

Figure 3.22 The graphic element on the left is flipped along the X-axis.

Figure 3.23 Right-clicking a selected object displays a menu containing the option to convert the element to a path.

Converting a Graphic Element to a Path

If you have drawn or imported vector-based artwork in Blend, you may need to edit individual points within the graphic element to finesse its look and feel. In this section, you convert a graphic element to a path.

To convert a graphic element to a path:

1. Select an element on the Artboard.

2. Right-click the element, and choose Path > Convert to Path (**Figure 3.23**).

   Or:

   From Blend's main menu, choose Object > Path > Convert to Path.

Distorting Graphic Elements

After converting an object to a path, you have much more freedom to distort that object. In the following examples, you distort a rectangle.

To perform the following steps, first draw a rectangle on the Artboard and convert it to a path (see the previous section, "Converting a Graphic Element to a Path").

To move the edges:

1. From the Toolbox, choose the Direct Selection tool; then, on the Artboard, select the rectangle path.

2. Position the pointer over an edge of the rectangle. The pointer changes to an arrow with a curved line to indicate that you can move the edge (**Figure 3.24**).

3. Drag the edge to reposition it (**Figure 3.25**). **Figure 3.26** shows the resulting rectangle.

Figure 3.24 The pointer changes when you position it next to the path's edge, indicating that the edge can be moved.

Figure 3.25 The original rectangle remains visible while you reposition the edge.

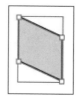

Figure 3.26 After releasing the mouse button, you can see the distorted rectangle.

Figure 3.27 Holding down the [Alt] key while the pointer is on the edge changes the pointer to a half-arrow with a curved line.

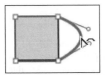

Figure 3.28 The original rectangle remains visible while you curve the edge.

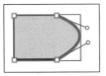

Figure 3.29 A rectangle with a curved edge.

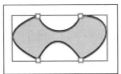

Figure 3.30 An example of a rectangle with all its edges curved. Notice that the nodes remain in their original positions.

To curve the edges:

1. From the Toolbox, choose the Direct Selection tool; then, on the Artboard, select the rectangle path.

2. Hold down the [Alt] key while positioning the pointer over an edge of the rectangle path. The pointer changes to a half-arrow with a curved line to indicate that you can curve the edge (**Figure 3.27**).

3. Drag the edge to curve it (**Figure 3.28**).

   Figure 3.29 shows the resulting rectangle, and **Figure 3.30** show an example of the rectangle with all its edges curved.

DISTORTING GRAPHIC ELEMENTS

To move a node:

1. From the Toolbox, choose the Direct Selection tool; then, on the Artboard, select the rectangle path.

2. Position the pointer over a node of the rectangle. The pointer changes to an arrow with a dot to indicate that you can move the node (**Figure 3.31**).

3. Drag the node to move it (**Figure 3.32**).

   Figure 3.33 shows the resulting rectangle, and **Figure 3.34** shows an example of the rectangle with all its nodes repositioned.

Figure 3.31 Positioning the pointer over a node changes the pointer to an arrow with a dot.

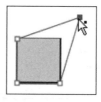

Figure 3.32 Dragging a node previews the rectangle's final appearance.

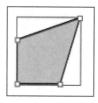

Figure 3.33 The rectangle's appearance after releasing the mouse button.

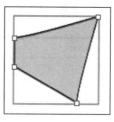

Figure 3.34 A rectangle with all its nodes repositioned.

Figure 3.35 Positioning the pointer over a node while holding down the [Alt] key changes the pointer to a half-arrow with a dot.

Figure 3.36 Dragging the node previews the curve of the edge.

Figure 3.37 The rectangle's appearance after releasing the mouse button.

Figure 3.38 A rectangle with all itsedges curved. Notice that the four nodes are still in the same places. Curving the edges does not reposition them.

To curve an edge using a node:

1. From the Toolbox, choose the Direct Selection tool; then, on the Artboard, select the rectangle path.

2. Hold down the [Alt] key while positioning the pointer over a node of the rectangle. The pointer changes to a half-arrow with a dot to indicate that you can curve the edge (**Figure 3.35**).

3. Drag the node to curve the edge (**Figure 3.36**).

   Figure 3.37 shows the resulting rectangle, and **Figure 3.38** shows an example of the rectangle with all its edges curved.

Creating a Triangle

By using the basic shapes available in Blend's Toolbox, you can create complex geometric shapes. Applying principles used earlier in this chapter—such as selecting, converting objects to paths, and rotating—you can create a triangle.

1. On the Artboard, draw a rectangle (**Figure 3.39**).

2. Convert the rectangle to a path (**Figure 3.40**).

3. From the Toolbox, choose the Direct Selection tool. Click the upper right node of the rectangle (**Figure 3.41**).

4. Press the Del key. This deletes the node and redraws the line between the upper left node and the lower right node, creating a triangle (**Figure 3.42**).

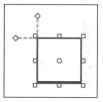

Figure 3.39 A base rectangle.

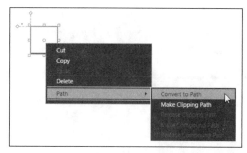

Figure 3.40 Right-clicking the rectangle gives you the option to convert it to a path.

Figure 3.41 Click the upper right node.

Figure 3.42 Pressing the Del key removes the node, creating a triangle.

WORKING WITH GRAPHIC LAYOUTS AND GROUPS

4

Layout panels, such as Grids and Canvases, are the foundation of Silverlight and WPF applications. They act as containers for visual elements. By default, layout panels are adaptive in nature. For example, when you build an interface, the panel automatically adjusts to the size of the window.

Layout panels also allow you to apply transforms. This capability is useful when animating a group of visual elements, because the animation is applied to the layout panel and not to each individual element.

In this chapter, you'll learn about the types of layout panels in Silverlight 2 and how to use them.

✔ Tip

■ For more about transforms, see Chapter 3.

Selecting the Correct Layout Panel

In Blend, the main layout panels are the Grid, Canvas, Stack, Wrap, and Dock panels. (Note that the Wrap and Dock panels are specific to WPF.) You select a panel based on how you want the elements in the panel to appear.

Table 4.1

Layout Panel Types	
LAYOUT PANEL	BEHAVIOR
Grid	Visual elements are arranged in rows and columns. See "Working with the Grid Panel."
Canvas	Visual elements are arranged in fixed positions. See "Working with the Canvas Panel."
Stack	Visual elements are arranged in a horizontal or vertical line. See "Working with the Stack Panel."
Wrap (WPF only)	Like the Stack panel, the Wrap panel arranges items in a single line. Unlike the Stack panel, the Wrap panel wraps items to a new line when they run out of room.
Dock (WPF only)	Visual elements lock to the edge of the panel.

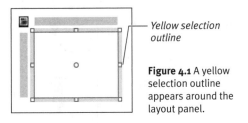

Yellow selection outline

Figure 4.1 A yellow selection outline appears around the layout panel.

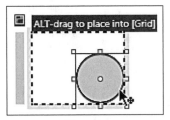

Figure 4.2 The tooltip displayed over the layout panel.

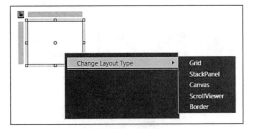

Figure 4.3 The context menu for a layout panel.

General Layout Panel Actions

All panel types can be manipulated in similar ways using tools in the Toolbox. In this section, you will choose panel types, add elements to panels, and change one panel type to another.

To make a panel active:

1. Draw a layout panel of any type on the Artboard.

2. From the Toolbox, choose the Selection tool.

3. Double-click the panel. A yellow outline appears, to indicate that the panel is selected (**Figure 4.1**).

To add an element to a panel:

1. Draw both an object and a layout panel on the Artboard.

2. From the Toolbox, choose the Selection tool.

3. Click the object and drag it to the layout panel. A dotted line outlines the layout panel, and a tooltip, "ALT-drag to place into," appears (**Figure 4.2**). Hold down the [Alt] key while dragging the control to place the object in the layout panel.

To change a panel type:

1. Draw a layout panel on the Artboard.

2. From the Toolbox, choose the Selection tool.

3. Right-click the layout panel and choose Change Layout Type. From the context menu, choose the new layout type (**Figure 4.3**).

Working with the Grid Panel

The Grid panel is the most versatile panel style because of its flexible layout. Elements in the Grid can grow to the size of the Grid and align themselves to the edges or center of the panel, unlike the Canvas panel, which locks elements in fixed positions.

Rows and columns

Rows and columns organize the Grid panel into logical areas.

To add a row or column:

1. From the Toolbox, choose the Grid tool and draw a Grid on the Artboard.

2. From the Toolbox, choose the Selection tool.

3. Double-click the Grid. A yellow selection outline appears around the edges of the Grid along with rulers to the top and left sides (**Figure 4.4**).

4. To add a column, position the mouse pointer over the top ruler. The pointer changes to an arrow with a plus sign, and an orange preview line appears where the column will be inserted (**Figure 4.5**). Click the ruler to add the new column.

5. To add a row, position the mouse pointer over the left ruler. As when adding a column, the pointer changes and a preview line appears to indicate where a new row will be placed (**Figure 4.6**). Click the ruler to add a new row.

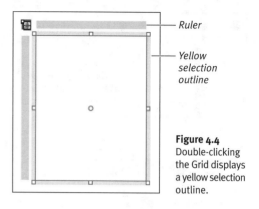

Ruler

Yellow selection outline

Figure 4.4
Double-clicking the Grid displays a yellow selection outline.

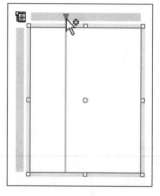

Figure 4.5
Positioning the mouse pointer over the top ruler changes the pointer and displays a preview line to indicate where the column separator will be placed.

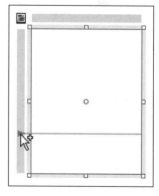

Figure 4.6
Positioning the mouse pointer over the left ruler changes the pointer and displays a preview line to indicate where the row separator will be placed.

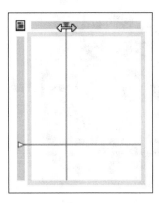

Figure 4.7
Positioning the mouse pointer over the column indicator changes the cursor, indicating you can select the column.

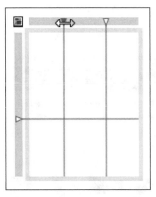

Figure 4.8 The pointer becomes a double arrow when the pointer is positioned over a column line in the ruler.

To remove a row or column:

1. Using the Selection tool, double-click the Grid on the Artboard.

2. Position the mouse pointer over a row or column indicator in the ruler. The pointer changes to a left/right arrow when the pointer is positioned over the row/column indicator (**Figure 4.7**).

3. Click the indicator and press the ⌈Del⌋ key.
   Or:
   Double-click the line.

To change the width of a row or column:

1. Using the Selection tool, double-click the Grid on the Artboard.

2. Position the pointer over a column or row separator. The pointer changes to a left/right arrow to indicate that you can move the line (**Figure 4.8**).

3. Drag the line to adjust the row or column to the desired size.

Positioning elements in a Grid panel

In Chapter 3, you positioned elements using the Selection tool and by modifying the transform. In this section, you'll position elements in a Grid panel using the alignment tools and modifying the Margin properties.

To position an object using the alignment tools:

1. Create a Grid and draw an object in it.

2. Using the Selection tool, click the object on the Artboard.

3. In the Properties panel, locate the Layout section. This section contains buttons to set the horizontal alignment and vertical alignment (**Figure 4.9**). The default value for HorizontalAlignment and VerticalAlignment is Stretch, the far right button.

4. To change the alignment, click one of the setting buttons. Buttons for Horizontal-Alignment are Left, Center, Right, and Stretch (**Figure 4.10**). Buttons for Vertical-Alignment are Top, Center, Bottom, and Stretch (**Figure 4.11**).

Figure 4.12 shows a circle with a value of 50 for Width and Height, Margin values of zero, and two different alignments. To align to the edge, the margins must be set to zero. Equally important, assigning a static size to your object ensures that the object won't disappear. Sizing is further covered below in the section "Understanding sizes in a Grid panel."

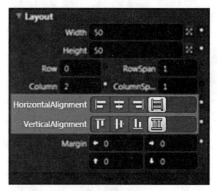

Figure 4.9 HorizontalAlignment and VerticalAlignment setting buttons are found in the Layout section of the Properties panel.

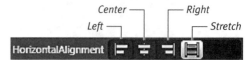

Figure 4.10 Buttons for HorizontalAlignment are Left, Center, Right, and Stretch.

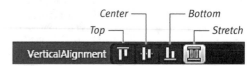

Figure 4.11 Buttons for VerticalAlignment are Top, Center, Bottom, and Stretch.

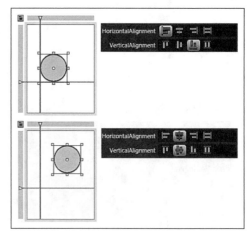

Figure 4.12 The top circle is aligned to the left and bottom. The bottom circle is aligned to the center, horizontally and vertically.

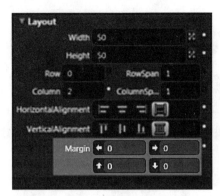

Figure 4.13 Margin values are found in the Layout section of the Properties panel.

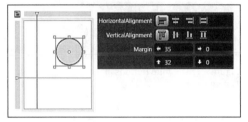

Figure 4.14 The circle is aligned to the top left with a top margin value of 32 and a left margin value of 35.

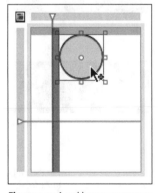

Figure 4.15 A red bumper appears when you move the circle to the edge of the Grid.

To position an object by changing the margin values:

1. Create a Grid and draw an object in it.

2. Using the Selection tool, click the object on the Artboard.

3. In the Properties panel, locate the Layout section. In this section, you can modify the margin values (**Figure 4.13**).

4. To change the margin values, in the Margin area enter new values, in clockwise order, for Left, Right, Bottom, and/or Top. As you change the values, the object updates on the Artboard.

Figure 4.14 shows a circle aligned to the top left with a top margin of 32 and a left margin of 35. Margins are relative to the object alignment.

✔ Tip

■ A red bumper appears when you move an object next to the Grid's edge (**Figure 4.15**). This visual aid indicates that you are close to the edge, and a margin value of 8 is applied to the object.

WORKING WITH THE GRID PANEL

Understanding sizes in a Grid panel

Elements in the Grid can be sized dynamically by setting the Width and Height values to Auto. As the Grid expands and shrinks, the contained elements resize automatically. To preserve the design integrity, you can constrain the height and width to minimum and maximum values.

To set the width and height to autosize:

1. Create a Grid and draw an object in it.

2. Using the Selection tool, click the object on the Artboard.

3. In the Properties panel, locate the Layout section. In this section, you can change the width and height values (**Figure 4.16**).

4. To the right of the Width and Height fields are buttons to set those values to Auto (**Figure 4.17**). Click the button to set the value to Auto for the respective property.

Figure 4.18 shows a circle before and after the Auto value is applied. The Alignment properties must be set to Stretch to enable the dynamic layout capability.

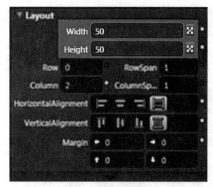

Figure 4.16 Width and height values are found in the Layout section of the Properties panel.

Figure 4.17 The Auto buttons in the Layout section.

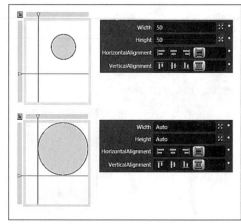

Figure 4.18 The circle stretches to the size of the cell after the Height and Width values are set to Auto.

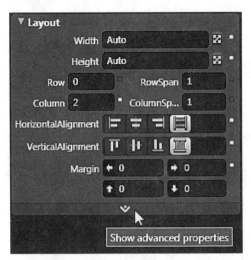

Figure 4.19 Expanding the Layout section's properties view.

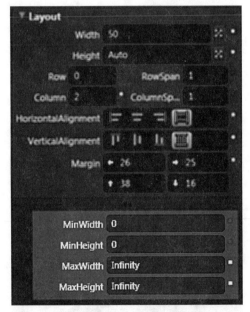

Figure 4.20 MinWidth, MinHeight, MaxWidth, and MaxHeight fields are located in the advanced properties.

To set minimum and maximum values for width and height:

1. Create a Grid and draw an object in it.

2. Using the Selection tool, click the object on the Artboard.

3. In the Properties panel, locate the Layout section. At the bottom of the section, click the down-arrow button to show advanced properties (**Figure 4.19**).

4. The advanced properties area reveals the values for MinWidth, MinHeight, MaxWidth, and MaxHeight (**Figure 4.20**). Enter new values in the data fields to set these values.

Working with the Canvas Panel

The Canvas panel is the simplest of the layout panels. In contrast to the Grid, the Canvas supports absolute positioning only. Elements do not automatically resize or align.

To position objects in a Canvas panel:

1. From the Toolbox, choose the Canvas tool 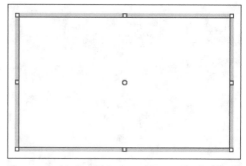 and draw a Canvas on the Artboard.

2. From the Toolbox, choose the Selection tool.

3. Double-click the Canvas object on the Artboard. A yellow outline appears around the edges of the Canvas (**Figure 4.21**).

4. Draw an object in the Canvas (**Figure 4.22**).

5. To position the object:

   Use the Selection tool to move the object. (See Chapter 2 for more information on how to move an object using the Selection tool.)

   Or:

   In the Layout section of the Properties panel, modify the values for Left and Top (**Figure 4.23**). As the values change, the object on the Artboard moves to reflect the change.

Figure 4.21 A selected Canvas object on the Artboard.

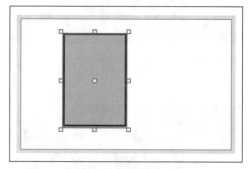

Figure 4.22 A rectangle drawn in a Canvas.

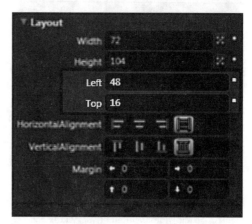

Figure 4.23 To position objects in a Canvas, change the values for Left and Top.

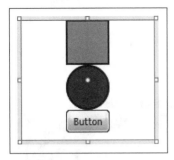

Figure 4.24 Three objects drawn in a Stack panel.

Figure 4.25 The Orientation pop-up menu in the Layout section of the Properties panel.

Working with the Stack Panel

As the name suggests, the Stack panel stacks its containing elements into a single line. As with the Grid panel, the widths and heights can be set dynamically.

To change the orientation of the Stack panel:

1. From the Toolbox, choose the StackPanel tool 📧 and draw a Stack panel on the Artboard.

2. From the Toolbox, choose the Selection tool.

3. Double-click the Stack panel on the Artboard. Draw a few objects in the Stack panel (**Figure 4.24**).

4. By default, the orientation of elements within a Stack panel is vertical. To change the orientation, select the Stack panel. In the Layout section of the Properties panel, from the Orientation pop-up menu, choose Horizontal (**Figure 4.25**).

Grouping Graphic Elements

In Blend, you can group two or more objects in a layout panel. Grouping elements enables you to more easily transform, move, or select objects that are related to one another.

To group objects into a panel:

1. Select the objects you want to group.

2. From the main application menu, choose Objects > Group Into, and choose the layout panel type you would like to group the objects into.

   Or:

   Right-click the selected objects, and from the context menu, choose Group Into; then choose the layout panel type you desire (**Figure 4.26**).

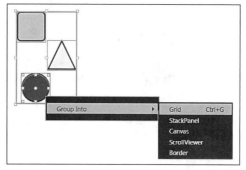

Figure 4.26 After selecting a group of objects, right-click to group the objects into a new layout panel.

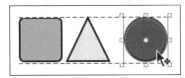

Figure 4.27 A red dotted line appears when objects are aligned.

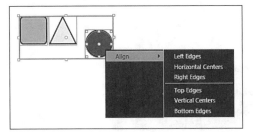

Figure 4.28 The context menu for a group of selected objects.

Aligning Graphic Elements

You can also align elements to one another in a layout panel.

To align objects:

1. Create two or more objects on the Artboard.

2. Using the Selection tool, drag one of the objects. As you drag the object closer to other objects, a red dotted line will appear (**Figure 4.27**). The dotted line indicates that the objects are aligning.

   Or:

   Select two or more objects on the Artboard. From the application menu, choose Objects > Align, and then choose how you want to align the objects. You can also open this menu by right-clicking the selected objects on the Artboard (**Figure 4.28**).

ALIGNING GRAPHIC ELEMENTS

Ordering Graphic Elements

Objects that are listed lower in the Objects and Timeline panel and in XAML are layered in front of other objects (**Figure 4.29**). This behavior is a major difference between Blend and other graphics programs that present layer order in a top down fashion.

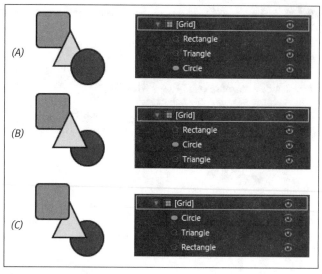

Figure 4.29 Three objects with three different orders. (A) The circle is lower in the Objects and Timeline panel displaying it on top. (B) The triangle is lower in the Objects and Timeline panel displaying it on top. (C) The rectangle is lower in the Objects and Timeline panel displaying it visually on top.

Working with Resources

Resources in Blend are objects that allow you to reuse values of properties. For example, colors and styles tend to be properties that are used throughout a design. Creating and applying these properties as a resource decreases the time you spend building an application's user interface and ensures a consistent look and feel. In this chapter, you create, edit, and apply resources.

Like previous chapters, this chapter focuses on resources related to Silverlight 2 projects.

Understanding Resources

The first question to be asked is: what properties can be made into resources? The answer is: almost any property. Most properties in the Properties panel have a button located at the end of their values. The button indicates that the property can use advanced options. One such option is to convert the value to a resource. **Table 5.1** shows the three types of properties that can be converted into a resource.

Scope of a resource

The *scope* of a resource determines the level where that resource can be used in an application. **Table 5.2** shows the levels of scope within which a resource can be defined.

Table 5.1

Types of Properties

PROPERTY	DESCRIPTION
Brushes	Known as color properties. Values include Fill, Stroke, and OpacityMask.
Properties	General properties, such as double values used for width, height, or transforms; Thickness properties used for Margins; or Enumeration properties such as HorizontalAlignment and VerticalAlignment.
Styles	Visual styles for controls can also be made into resources. Creating custom control styles is covered in Chapter 8.

Table 5.2

Scope of Resources

SCOPE	DESCRIPTION
Object	The resource is created only for the object and its children.
Document	Resources are stored in the same page as the object and can be applied only to objects in the same document.
Application	Resources are stored in the App.xaml file at the root of the application and can be applied to any object in the application.
Resource dictionary	(WPF only) Resources are stored in a separate file and can be applied to the entire application, much like Application-level resources. The advantage of using resource dictionaries is the ability to port them between applications.

Figure 5.1 The "Advanced property options" buttons in the Properties panel.

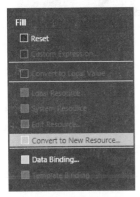

Figure 5.2 Choose Convert to New Resource from the context menu.

Figure 5.3 Click the Brush button to create a new brush resource.

Creating a Resource

Most properties can be converted to a resource. In the following section, you learn how to create brush resources, as they are the most complex. You can use similar techniques to create other properties as a resource.

To create a brush resource:

1. Create an object or select an object on the Artboard.

2. In the Properties panel, click the "Advanced property options" button next to a property. **Figure 5.1** shows the button next to the Stroke property.

3. *Do one of the following:*

   In the context Advanced Property Options menu, select the Convert to New Resource check box (**Figure 5.2**). Make sure the Brush you are trying to create does not have the value of "No brush." Otherwise, the menu option of Convert to New Resource will be grayed out.

   Or:

   In the Properties panel, at the bottom of the Brushes section, click the Brush button (**Figure 5.3**) to open the Create Brush Resource dialog.

   Continues on next page

4. In the Create Brush Resource dialog, enter a value for the Name (Key), and choose where you would like the resource defined from the "Define in" options, Application and "This document" (**Figure 5.4**). (See the tip at the end of this section for more information on these location options.)

You can quickly distinguish properties using resources from local values by the green outline around the property (**Figure 5.5**).

✔ Tip

■ When creating resources, it's best to define them at the application level. There, the resources are placed in a central location and accessible from any page in the project. Defining a resource at the document level or the object level constrains the resource to a narrower scope.

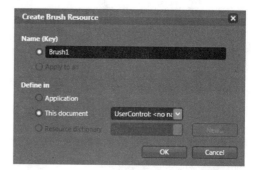

Figure 5.4 Enter a Name for the new resource you're creating.

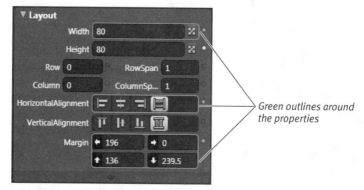

Green outlines around the properties

Figure 5.5 Green outlines appear around values with resources applied.

Figure 5.6 To display the resources for the brush, select the "Brush resources" tab.

Figure 5.7 The "Brush resources" tab lists all available resources of that specific type.

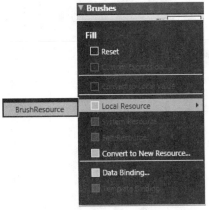

Figure 5.8 The submenu under Local Resource lists available resources for the property.

Applying Resources to Objects

After you have created a resource, you can use that resource with one or more objects in your application. Remember, by creating a resource, you have the flexibility to change the resource parameters, affecting any and all objects that use that resource.

To apply a brush resource:

There are three ways to apply a resource to a brush. Before you try one of these three methods, create an object or select an object from the Artboard.

Do one of the following:

1. In the Brushes section of the Properties panel, choose a brush. Then click the "Brush resources" tab (**Figure 5.6**).

2. Expand the Local Brush Resources list, and choose a resource to apply to the brush object (**Figure 5.7**).

Or:

1. In the Properties panel, in the Brushes section, click the "Advanced property options" button next to a brush property such as Fill, Stroke, or OpacityMask.

2. In the "Advanced property options" menu, select a resource from the Local Resource submenu, as shown in **Figure 5.8**.

Continues on next page

Continues on next page

APPLYING RESOURCES TO OBJECTS

Or:

1. Open the Resources panel (**Figure 5.9**).

2. Drag a resource from the Resources panel onto an object on the Artboard (**Figure 5.10**).

3. When you release the mouse button, a context menu appears, based on the type of resource you are trying to apply (**Figure 5.11**). Choose the property to which you want to apply the resource.

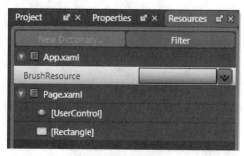

Figure 5.9 Select a resource from the Resources panel.

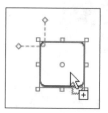

Figure 5.10 Drag the resource onto an object on the Artboard.

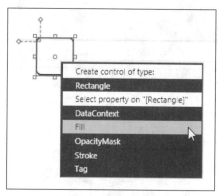

Figure 5.11 The menu shows the properties to which you can apply the resource.

Figure 5.12 Choose Edit Resource from the Advanced Property Options menu.

Figure 5.13 The Edit Resource dialog.

Figure 5.14 The Resources panel enables you to directly edit resources.

Editing a Resource

You may need to create a resource before you have finalized a style guide or design specification for an application. Therefore, you need the flexibility to edit a resource if changes need to be made to the look and feel of the application. In this section, you'll modify an existing resource.

To edit a brush resource:

There are two ways to edit a resource. Before you try one of these methods, create an object or select an object from the Artboard.

Do one of the following:

1. In the Properties panel, click the "Advanced property options" button next to a property that has a resource applied.

2. From the context menu that opens, choose Edit Resource (**Figure 5.12**).

3. In the Edit Resource dialog that opens, you can change the values for the resource (**Figure 5.13**).

Or:

1. Click the Resources panel tab (next to the Properties panel).

2. In the Resources panel, you will find a list of resources available in the application (**Figure 5.14**). You can directly edit the values for those resources. For some values, an arrow button is located at the end of the text box. Click the arrow button to display additional values for the resource.

EDITING A RESOURCE

CREATING
BASIC ANIMATIONS

6

The inclusion of the animation engine to Silverlight 2 and WPF enables you to add motion graphics to your application without using third-party plug-ins. More important, because the animation engine is native to Silverlight/WPF, Blend can provide a rich animation workspace.

Blend uses keyframes to structure animations. Keyframes are frames in the timeline that contain information about an object's value at that given time. The animation system interpolates values over time, meaning you do not have to create frame-by-frame animations. You simply create keyframes to define a range of motion or values, and the animation system does the heavy lifting for you.

Properties such as color, position, scale, and rotation are commonly animated. However, Blend does not limit you to these properties. Virtually any object's properties can be manipulated over time, including nonvisual properties.

Touring the Timeline Panel

In previous chapters, you worked with the Objects and Timeline section of the Interactions panel, but your work was restricted to objects. In this chapter, you'll explore the second part of the panel: the timeline.

In the timeline, you create and preview animations. Before viewing a timeline, you have to create one. **Figure 6.1** shows the Objects and Timeline panel when it's populated with animations.

The Timeline options menu

An important menu in the Timeline section is the options menu. This menu enables you to create, duplicate, reverse, delete, rename, or close the animations in a timeline (**Table 6.1**). You can open the menu by clicking the drop-down button to the right of the New button (**Figure 6.2**).

✔ Tip

- As you learned in Chapter 1, Blend provides an environment specifically for animations, the Animation Workspace. This chapter uses this workspace to better demonstrate the timeline. To open the Animation Workspace, choose Window > Active Workspace > Animation Workspace, or press F6.

Table 6.1

Timeline Options Menu	
OPTION	DESCRIPTION
New	Creates a new timeline.
Duplicate	Copies the current timeline to a new timeline.
Reverse	Switches the timeline beginning and ending values.
Delete	Enables you to rename a timeline.
Rename	The text equivalent of the supplied time
Close	Stops the environment from recording animations and closes the current timeline.

Figure 6.1 The Objects and Timeline panel with an active timeline.

Figure 6.2 The Timeline options menu.

Figure 6.3 Choose New from the options menu to create a new timeline.

Figure 6.4 The Create Storyboard Resource dialog.

Figure 6.5 The red outlines indicate you are recording values.

Red dot indicates a timeline is recording

Figure 6.6 The Objects and Timeline panel with an active timeline.

Working with Timelines

A timeline defines animations, or any content manipulated over time. Generally, timelines include related animations, such as the fading in and out of interface elements or transitions between application states. In this exercise, you will create, open, rename, duplicate, and delete timelines.

To create a timeline:

1. In the Objects and Timeline section of the Interaction panel, click the New button [+].
   Or:
   Click the drop-down button next to the New timeline button to open the options menu and choose New (**Figure 6.3**).

2. In the Create Storyboard Resource dialog box, enter a name for the timeline and click OK (**Figure 6.4**).
   After you close the Create Storyboard Resource dialog box, the Blend interface changes in two ways:
   ▲ The Artboard is outlined in red and "Timeline recording is on" appears in the upper-left corner (**Figure 6.5**).
   ▲ The timeline appears in the Objects and Timeline panel, and the timeline name is placed in the text box under the section head. A red dot to the left of the name indicates that the timeline is recording (**Figure 6.6**).

To open or change a timeline:

◆ In the Objects and Timeline panel, directly under the Objects and Timeline section head, click the Open a Storyboard button, next to the text box. **Figure 6.7** shows a list of timelines previously created. By default, the text box displays "(No Storyboard open)". Clicking the button opens a menu of available timelines. In this menu, you can search through your timelines, just like searching the Asset Library, discussed in Chapter 2.

To delete a timeline:

Deleting a timeline in Blend is easy to do, but be careful. There is no confirmation message asking to prevent you from mistakenly deleting a timeline. This can be very frustrating, but you are in luck. The undo functionality saves the day. Perform an undo by either pressing Ctrl Z or choosing Edit > Undo.

1. Open the timeline you wish to delete.

2. From the Timeline options menu, choose Delete (**Figure 6.8**).

To duplicate a timeline:

1. Open the timeline you want to copy.

2. From the options menu, choose Duplicate (**Figure 6.9**).

   You are now working in the duplicated timeline. Also, the duplicate timeline name is given a suffix of _Copy1_ so that you can easily distinguish the duplicate from the original (**Figure 6.10**).

Figure 6.7 The menu of available timelines.

Figure 6.8 The Delete item in the Timeline options menu.

Figure 6.9 The Duplicate item in the Timeline options menu.

Figure 6.10 The newly created duplicate timeline has a _Copy1_ suffix added to its name.

Figure 6.11 Choose Reverse from the options menu.

(A)

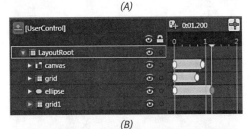

(B)

Figure 6.12 (A) A series of animations before applying Reverse. (B) The resulting animations after applying Reverse.

Figure 6.13 Choose Rename from the options menu.

Figure 6.14 The timeline's name is highlighted and ready to be renamed.

To reverse a timeline:

1. Open the timeline containing the animated content you want to reverse.

2. From the options menu, choose Reverse (**Figure 6.11**).

3. The start and end points of the timeline are switched and the animations in the timeline are reversed. **Figure 6.12** shows before and after views of a reversed timeline.

To rename a timeline:

1. Open the timeline you want to rename.

2. From the options menu, choose Rename (**Figure 6.13**).

3. The current timeline's name is highlighted, indicating that you can edit the name (**Figure 6.14**).

To close a Storyboard:

◆ Next to the Storyboard name in the Objects
and Timeline panel, click the Close
Storyboard button  (**Figure 6.15**).
Or:

◆ Choose the Close item from the Timeline
options menu (**Figure 6.16**).

Figure 6.15 Click the Close Storyboard
button to stop recording animations.

Figure 6.16 The Close item in the
Timeline options menu.

What Is a Storyboard?

Timelines created in Blend are represented in XAML as Storyboards. For each animation
created on the timeline, an XAML representation is added to the Storyboard. **Figure 6.17**
shows an example of a Storyboard in XAML.

```
<Storyboard x:Name="FadeIn">
    <DoubleAnimationUsingKeyFrames BeginTime="00:00:00"
        Storyboard.TargetName="grid1" Storyboard.TargetProperty="(UIElement.Opacity)">
        <SplineDoubleKeyFrame KeyTime="00:00:00" Value="0"/>
        <SplineDoubleKeyFrame KeyTime="00:00:01" Value="1"/>
    </DoubleAnimationUsingKeyFrames>
</Storyboard>
```

Figure 6.17 XAML representation of a timeline.

Figure 6.18 The Record Keyframe button on the timeline.

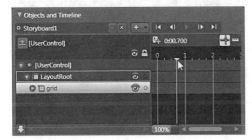

Figure 6.19 Drag the playhead along the timeline.

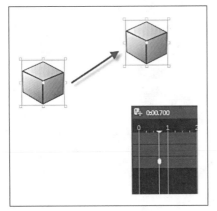

Figure 6.20 Moving an object on the Artboard creates a keyframe on the timeline.

Working with Keyframes

Keyframes are points in an animation that define a state of an object at a specified time. When you need to make a significant change to an object's property, you should create a keyframe at the point in the timeline where you want that change to occur. A keyframe is usually located at the beginning and end of an animation, but you can add keyframes anywhere, as necessary.

To record a new keyframe:

1. Open a timeline.

2. Select the objects you want to animate. To select multiple objects, press [Ctrl] while clicking individual objects.

3. Add a keyframe by *doing one of the following:*

   ▲ Click the Record Keyframe button, located at the upper-left corner of the timeline (**Figure 6.18**).

   Or:

   ▲ In the timeline, drag the yellow playhead to the time you want your animation to end (**Figure 6.19**). Then, modify a property of that selected object. **Figure 6.20** shows how moving an object on the Artboard creates a keyframe on the timeline.

✔ Tip

■ If you want the animation to begin at its current location, create a keyframe by clicking the Record Keyframe button. Otherwise, create a keyframe by moving the playhead to the end point of your animation and then modify one or more properties. You might find this second method a faster and more intuitive way to create a keyframe.

WORKING WITH KEYFRAMES

To move a keyframe:

1. Open a timeline that includes animations.

2. Click a keyframe and drag it along the timeline to a new location, as shown in **Figure 6.21**.

To remove a keyframe:

1. Open a timeline that includes animations.

2. *Do one of the following:*

   ▲ Click a keyframe to select it, and press ⎡Del⎤.

   Or:

   ▲ Right-click the keyframe and choose Delete from the context menu (**Figure 6.22**).

Figure 6.21 Drag a keyframe to reposition it.

Figure 6.22 Choosing Delete from the context menu for a keyframe in a timeline.

Figure 6.23 The Playback controls.

Figure 6.24 Click Play to play your animation.

Previewing an Animation

When you edit a timeline, Playback controls are located to the right of the timeline name in the Objects and Timeline panel (**Figure 6.23**). These controls enable you to go to the first frame, go to the previous frame, play the animation, go to the next frame, and go to the last frame.

To preview an animation:

1. Open a timeline that includes animations.

2. The timeline playhead is positioned at zero seconds. Click the Play button to start the animation (**Figure 6.24**). A time-lapse view of an animation on the Artboard is shown in **Figure 6.25**.

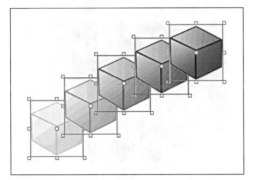

Figure 6.25 The movement of an object across the Artboard.

Adding Easing

Adding acceleration and deceleration to some animations can lend a more natural look to playback. To achieve this effect in Blend, you modify the easing values for a keyframe.

To add easing to a keyframe:

1. Click a keyframe to select it.

2. Click the Properties panel to display the properties for that keyframe (**Figure 6.26**).

3. *Do one of the following:*

   ▲ Drag the lower-left dot or the upper-right dot until you create the desired easing curve (**Figure 6.27**).

   Or:

   ▲ Right-click a keyframe.

   In the context menu, the Ease In and Ease Out options include predefined easing values ranging from 0% to 100%. Select one of these values to apply easing to the keyframe (**Figure 6.28**). To see the effect of applying an easing value this way, see the results in the Easing section of the Properties panel.

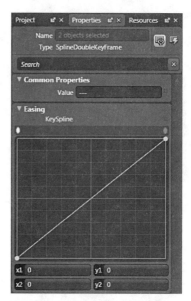

Figure 6.26 The Properties panel for a keyframe.

Figure 6.27 Dragging the lower-left dot to change the easing curve.

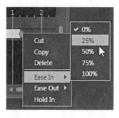

Figure 6.28 The easing options in the context menu of a keyframe on a timeline.

Figure 6.29 A selected object in the Objects and Timeline panel.

Figure 6.30 The timeline is named *AnimateColor*.

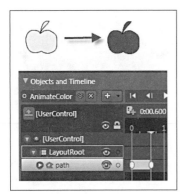

Figure 6.31 The final color-effect animation.

Animating Color Effects

Using the lessons in this section combined with those in previous chapters, you can now animate the color of an object. The animation of an object's color can serve a wide range of purposes: transitioning from one section of the application to another or enhancing creative expression within an application. Animating the color of an object can also help the user identify active and inactive elements of a user interface, where dimmed (or desaturated) elements are inactive and normal color-adjusted elements are active.

To animate the color property of an object:

1. Select an object from the Artboard or in the Objects and Timeline panel (**Figure 6.29**).

2. Create a new timeline and name it (**Figure 6.30**). Click OK.

3. Click the Record Keyframe button to set the initial state of the timeline.

4. Move the playhead to a new position.

5. Finally, change the color of the object in the Properties panel. **Figure 6.31** shows the resulting animation.

✔ Tip

■ Now that you know how to animate color, try animating other properties, such as an object's size (width and height) or rotation value.

ANIMATING COLOR EFFECTS

WORKING WITH IMAGES, VIDEO, AND AUDIO

7

One of the primary reasons to use Silverlight 2 to deploy content over the Internet is to deliver media-rich experiences to your audience using media that is not easily displayed or controlled in standard HTML. In this chapter, you'll import media files to your project and assign the media to controls that you've placed on the Artboard.

Media Formats

Blend supports a wide range of media file formats, as shown in **Table 7.1**. If you have an asset that is not in a supported format, you must use a graphics, audio, or video program to convert the asset to a supported format.

Table 7.1

Supported Formats	
MEDIA TYPE	SUPPORTED FORMATS
Images	BMP, GIF, ICO, JPEG, PNG, and TIFF
Audio	AIF, AIFC, AIFF, ASF, AU, MID, MIDI, MP2, MP3, MPA, MPE, RMI, SND, WAV, WMA, WMD
Video	ASF, AVI, DVR-MS, IFO, M1V, MPEG, MPG, VOB, WM, and WMV

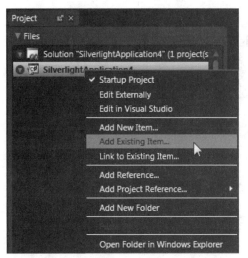

Figure 7.1 Right-click the project name to add media.

Figure 7.2 The Add Existing Item dialog.

Figure 7.3 Bear.wmv was added to the project by choosing Link to Existing Item, as indicated by the arrow over the icon.

Importing Images and Video

You can import media in Blend in two ways: add the media directly to the project, or create a link to the media, similar to the way a desktop shortcut icon points to an application.

To add media to a project:

1. In the Projects panel, right-click the project or a folder in your project. Where you click dictates the location to which the media is imported.

2. From the context menu, choose Add Existing Item or Link to Existing Item (**Figure 7.1**). To understand the difference between these choices, see the sidebar "What's the Difference Between Add Existing Item and Link to Existing Item?" later in this chapter.

3. If you chose Add Existing Item from the context menu, the Add Existing Item dialog will appear. Browse to the file you want to import and click Open (**Figure 7.2**).
   Or:
   If you chose Link to Existing Item from the context menu in step 2, the Link to Existing Item dialog will appear and the icon for the imported file name will have an arrow over it (**Figure 7.3**). This icon indicates that you have linked to the file and it is not physically embedded in your project.

What's the Difference Between Add Existing Item and Link to Existing Item?

When adding media, you can choose Add Existing Item or Link to Existing Item. Choosing Add Existing Item copies the file into your project and increases the overall file size of your project file. Choosing Link to Existing Item creates a shortcut in the project that points to the actual file.

If you link to an item, you need to copy the linked asset file(s) along with the deployed project files. There are a few reasons why you might link to an existing file. If you externalize assets, you can more easily swap linked assets at runtime. For example, if you are using a JPEG file as a placeholder for a photo that is still in production, you can update the linked JPEG file when the final image is ready. You can also minimize the loading time of your Silverlight project by linking external assets. Finally, some media files, such as video files, occupy a lot of hard disk storage space, and embedding the files into your project increases the necessary storage space on your system.

Figure 7.4 Search the Asset Library for the Image object.

Figure 7.5 An Image object drawn on the Artboard.

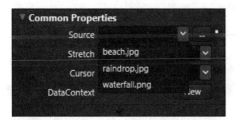

Figure 7.6 Select an image for the Source in Common Properties.

Figure 7.7 An Image object with the Source property set.

Working with Images

Bitmap images such as JPEG, PNG, and GIF files can be critical components in a successful user interface design. Blend enables you to easily place bitmap images in your Silverlight and WPF projects. In this section, you'll use the Image control to place graphics into your project.

To add an image:

1. After importing an image into your project, from the Toolbox, open the Asset Library. Search for the Image object (**Figure 7.4**), and select it.

2. Draw an Image object on the Artboard (**Figure 7.5**).

3. From the Common Properties section of the Properties panel, select an image for the Source property (**Figure 7.6**).

   After you set the Source property, the Artboard reflects the change (**Figure 7.7**).

✔ Tip

- You can also add an image to the Artboard by double-clicking the image in the Project panel or dragging it from the Project panel to the Artboard.

Creating an ImageBrush

Like application Resources (discussed in Chapter 5), an ImageBrush is nothing more than an Image Resource. It provides you with a way to reuse an image in multiple places. See "Advantages of an ImageBrush" later in this chapter for more information.

To create an ImageBrush:

1. Select an image from the Artboard or add a new image (**Figure 7.8**).

2. Choose Tools > Make Brush Resource > Make ImageBrush Resource (**Figure 7.9**).

3. In the Create ImageBrush Resource dialog, enter a name for the ImageBrush in the Name (Key) field and indicate whether you would like the ImageBrush to be defined in your application or only in the current document (**Figure 7.10**).

   The ImageBrush is now seen in the Resources panel. Notice that the ImageBrush includes a preview of the Image control (**Figure 7.11**).

Figure 7.8 A selected image.

Figure 7.9 Choose Tools > Make Brush Resource > Make ImageBrush Resource to create an ImageBrush.

Figure 7.10 The Create ImageBrush Resource dialog.

Figure 7.11 The Resources panel includes previews of the ImageBrush.

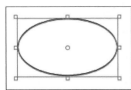

Figure 7.12 A selected ellipse.

Figure 7.13 The Brush resources tab.

Figure 7.14 Choose an ImageBrush from the Resources.

Figure 7.15 An ellipse with an ImageBrush applied.

To apply an ImageBrush to an object:

1. Select an object or draw one on the Artboard (**Figure 7.12**).

2. In the Brushes section of the Properties panel, select Fill, Stroke, or Opacity Mask, and click the "Brush resources" tab (**Figure 7.13**).

3. From the list of Resources, choose the ImageBrush resource (**Figure 7.14**) to apply the ImageBrush to the object (**Figure 7.15**). **Figure 7.16** shows the result of applying ImageBrushes to a variety of shapes.

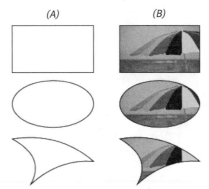

Figure 7.16 Column A shows a group of objects before an ImageBrush is applied. Column B shows the objects with an ImageBrush applied.

To apply an ImageBrush to text:

1. Select a TextBlock or draw one on the Artboard (**Figure 7.17**).

2. Convert the TextBlock to a path by choosing Object > Path > Convert to Path.

3. In the Brushes section of the Properties panel, change the Fill to an ImageBrush (**Figure 7.18**). (See "Creating an ImageBrush" earlier in this chapter for more information on the location of this option.)

To delete an ImageBrush:

1. Click the Resources panel.

2. Right-click the ImageBrush and choose Delete (**Figure 7.19**).

Figure 7.17 Draw a TextBlock on the Artboard.

Figure 7.18 Text after an ImageBrush is applied.

Figure 7.19 Delete the ImageBrush resource by choosing Delete from the context menu.

Advantages of an ImageBrush

If you need to use the same image with many objects, create an ImageBrush resource to optimize the use of that image. An ImageBrush resource renders the image once, and then applies the image to the object. In contrast, when you create an Image object without the use of an ImageBrush resource, the image data is duplicated in memory for each use, increasing the size of your application and potentially decreasing its performance.

CREATING AN IMAGEBRUSH

Figure 7.20 Search the Asset Library for the MediaElement object.

Figure 7.21 A MediaElement object drawn on the Artboard.

Figure 7.22 Choose a source file from the Source menu in the Media section of the Properties panel.

Figure 7.23 An Image object with the chosen source file.

Working with Audio and Video

In Blend, audio and video content is managed by the MediaElement control. The workflow is the same for audio and video assets. Only the sources are different.

To add video:

1. After importing an image into your project, from the Toolbox, open the Asset Library, and search for the MediaElement object (**Figure 7.20**). Select the object.

2. Draw a MediaElement object on the Artboard (**Figure 7.21**).

3. From the Source menu, located in the Media section of the Properties panel, choose a source video file (**Figure 7.22**).

   After you set the Source property, the Artboard reflects the change (**Figure 7.23**).

✔ Tip

■ You can also add a video to the Artboard is by double-clicking the video in the Project panel or dragging it from the Project panel to the Artboard.

Working with the Stretch Property

Both the MediaElement and the Image controls have a Stretch property, which enables you to control the aspect ratio of the media. This property is powerful because it makes working with media dimension very easy. The available Stretch properties are None, Fill, Uniform, and UniformToFill. **Table 7.2** describes how each property affects the media.

Table 7.2

Stretch Types

TYPE OF STRETCH	DESCRIPTION
None	The content keeps its original aspect ratio and dimensions (**Figure 7.24**).
Fill	The content is resized to fill the destination object but does not preserve the original aspect ratio (**Figure 7.25**).
Uniform	The content is resized to fit the destination object while preserving the original aspect ratio (**Figure 7.26**).
UniformToFill	The content is resized and, if necessary, cropped to fill the destination object while preserving the original aspect ratio. Content is cropped if the original aspect ratio does not match the destination object's aspect ratio (**Figure 7.27**).

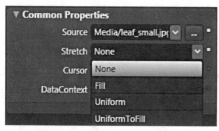

Figure 7.24 Stretch set to None.

Figure 7.25 Stretch set to Fill.

Figure 7.26 Stretch set to Uniform.

Figure 7.27 Stretch set to UniformToFill.

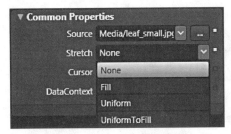

Figure 7.28 Select a new Stretch property in Common Properties.

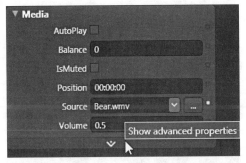

Figure 7.29 Accessing the advanced properties in the Media section of the Properties panel.

Figure 7.30 Select a Stretch property for the MediaElement control.

To set the Stretch property of an Image:

1. Choose an image, or draw one on the Artboard.

2. To change the Stretch property, in the Common Properties section of the Properties panel, choose an option from the Stretch menu (**Figure 7.28**).

To set the Stretch property of a MediaElement:

The following steps are applicable only to WPF and Silverlight 2 applications.

1. Draw or select a MediaElement object on the Artboard.

2. In the Media section of the Properties panel, click the down arrow to show the advanced properties (**Figure 7.29**).

3. From the Stretch menu, choose a Stretch property (**Figure 7.30**).

ImageBrush and Stretch

The ImageBrush also has the ability to define a Stretch property. The Stretch property of an ImageBrush is applied to any object using the ImageBrush. If you want an object with a Fill and another object with a Uniform stretch, you will need to create two ImageBrushes with different Stretch values.

To set the Stretch property of an ImageBrush resource:

1. In the Resources panel, click the down arrow next to the ImageBrush resource (**Figure 7.31**).

2. From the Stretch menu, choose a Stretch property (**Figure 7.32**).

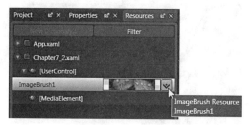

Figure 7.31 Click the Image next to the ImageBrush resource.

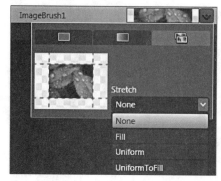

Figure 7.32 Change the Stretch property for the ImageBrush.

WORKING WITH THE STRETCH PROPERTY

Using the Markers Collection

Markers are embedded points placed in media to alert the playback component that an event is being called. Closed captioning and advertisements are examples of markers that could be embedded. In Blend, you can configure your own markers from the Markers Collection. To create a marker, you attach a text value to a specific time. The MediaPlayer will fire an event when the marker is reached. You will have to add logic to the code-behind file to handle this event.

Closed Captioning

Closed captioning text can be encoded in the video or placed in a separate file, usually in a SAMI (Synchronized Accessible Media Interchange) file format. If the captions are encoded into the video, the MediaElement control recognizes the captions as markers and can be programmatically displayed. Otherwise, you will have to program the interaction between the MediaElement control and the closed caption file.

To add markers to the Markers Collection:

1. Draw or select a Media element on the Artboard.

2. In the advanced properties area in the Media section of the Properties panel, click the button next to Markers (Collection) (**Figure 7.33**).

3. In the Markers dialog, click the "Add another item" button (**Figure 7.34**).

4. Enter Text, Time, and Type properties for the marker (**Figure 7.35**). The marker type is self-defined. It's important to know the marker type when you process the marker event in your code.

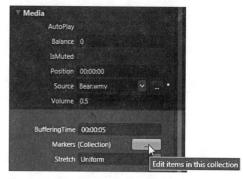

Figure 7.33 The Markers Collection is in the advanced properties area under Media.

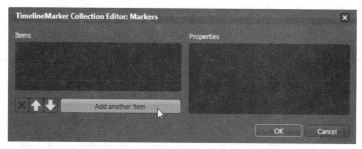

Figure 7.34 Click "Add another item" to add a marker.

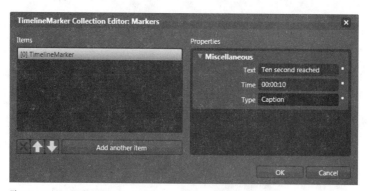

Figure 7.35 Enter Text, Time, and Type properties for the marker.

Styling
and Templates

Previous chapters covered fundamental controls such as Rectangle, Ellipse, Image, and MediaElement. Blend offers many more complex controls, such as Button, RadioButton, Slider, ProgressBar, and ComboBox, to name a few. Traditionally, it has been laboriously difficult to create consistent custom styles for controls within Windows programming. Silverlight 2 and WPF eliminate this barrier by providing ways to easily create and update styles. In this chapter, you will create and edit control styles.

Understanding Styles and Templates

In previous chapters, items on the Artboard were referred to as objects. This chapter focuses on a specific type of object, the *control*. A control goes beyond shapes and text, by extending the base functionality. Examples are the Button, CheckBox, DataGrid, and Slider controls.

Blend enables you to quickly encapsulate the look of a control in resources using styles and templates. After you create a style or template, you can apply it to controls of the same type.

What's the difference between a style and a template? Simply put, a style defines the default behavior of a control, and a template defines pieces of a control.

Styles are extremely useful when you want to change default properties such as height, width, background, stroke, and so on. You should create and apply templates when you want to overhaul the default look.

The Breadcrumb Bar

The breadcrumb bar offers a quick way to navigate between editing a style, a template, or the root in your project (**Figure 8.1**). It is located at the top-left corner of the Artboard. This bar appears only for controls that can have a style or template applied. You also can quickly add or edit styles using the breadcrumb bar.

Figure 8.1 The breadcrumb bar is located at the top-left corner of the Artboard.

Figure 8.2 Create a new style by choosing Object > Edit Style > Edit a Copy.

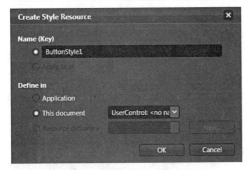

Figure 8.3 Enter a name for the new style in the Create Style Resource dialog.

Figure 8.4 Click the Scope Up button to exit the Edit Style mode.

Creating a Style

Styles are resources that define the look and feel of a control. The benefit of a style lies within its ability to define a look and then reuse it among multiple controls. Spending time to create a style can reduce your production time and increase the visual consistency of your application. (For more information, see Chapter 5, "Working with Resources.")

In the next exercise, you will create a style for a relatively simple control. The process of creating a style for a more complex control will be discussed later in this chapter. For now, you'll use a primitive shape such as a rectangle or ellipse.

To create a style:

1. Draw an object or select one from the Artboard.

2. Choose Object > Edit Style > Edit a Copy (**Figure 8.2**). (See the tip at the end of this exercise for a comparison of the Edit a Copy and Create Empty options.)

3. In the Create Style Resource dialog (**Figure 8.3**), enter a name for the new Style. Leave the "Define in" option set to "This document." Click OK to create the style.

   Your style is now created. Blend automatically displays the editing style mode. Any properties you can change in the Edit Style mode, such as Background color, Height, or Font size, are applied to the newly created Style.

4. To close the Edit Style mode, click the Scope Up button ⬆ in the Objects and Timeline panel (**Figure 8.4**).

Continues on next page

✔ Tip

■ Two options are available in the Object > Edit Style menu: Edit a Copy and Create Empty. Choosing Edit a Copy creates a duplicate Style based on the style of the currently selected object. Choosing Create Empty creates an empty style. When working with shapes and text controls, Create Empty is the only available option.

Using Editing Style Mode

After you create a style, Blend enters the editing style mode, or *edit scope*. Changes made to properties in this mode are applied to the style resource. You can quickly identify a control that has an applied style by the green outline placed around the Style property in the Miscellaneous section of the Properties panel (**Figure 8.5**).

Figure 8.5 A green outline appears around a Style property if the property is set.

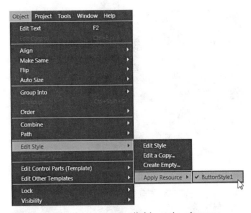

Figure 8.6 To choose an Available style, choose Object > Edit Style > Apply Resource.

Figure 8.7 The "Advanced property options" button.

To apply a style:

1. Draw an object or select one from the Artboard.

2. To apply the style, *do one of the following:*

   ▲ Choose Object > Edit Style > Apply Resource. A list of available styles appears for the control. Select a style to apply to the object (**Figure 8.6**).

   Or:

   ▲ In the Miscellaneous section of the Properties panel, click the "Advanced property options" button located next to the Style property (**Figure 8.7**).

3. From the "Advanced property options" menu, navigate to Local Resource, and choose the style you want to apply (**Figure 8.8**).

Figure 8.8 The "Advanced property options" menu.

Modifying a Style

After you have created and applied a style, you may need to change the style. In this section, you will edit a style.

To modify a style:

1. Draw an object or select one from the Artboard that has a style applied to it.

2. To modify the style, *do one of the following:*

   ▲ Choose Object > Edit Style > Edit Style (**Figure 8.9**).

   Or:

   ▲ In the Miscellaneous section of the Properties panel, click the Style property (**Figure 8.10**).

3. From the "Advanced property options" menu, choose Edit Resource (**Figure 8.11**).

   Blend displays the editing scope mode for that style. Just as when you create a style, any changes made in this mode are applied to the style. When you are working in the editing scope mode, the navigation bar includes an extra level for the style (**Figure 8.12**), and the Objects and Timeline panel displays the Edit Style mode (**Figure 8.13**).

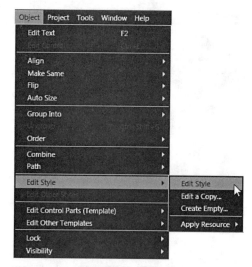

Figure 8.9 To edit a style, choose Object > Edit Style > Edit Style from the main menu.

Figure 8.10 Click the Style property to open the "Advanced property options" menu.

Figure 8.11 Choose Edit Resource from the "Advanced property options" menu.

Figure 8.12 The navigation bar indicates that you are editing a style.

Figure 8.13 The Objects and Timeline panel when editing a style.

Figure 8.14 The "Advanced property options" button for the Style property.

Figure 8.15 Choose the Reset option to remove the style from the control.

To remove a style:

1. Select an object with an applied style.

2. In the Miscellaneous section of the Properties panel, click the "Advanced property options" button for the Style property (**Figure 8.14**).

3. From the "Advanced property options" menu, choose Reset (**Figure 8.15**).

Creating a Template

Creating, applying, and editing templates is similar to working with styles. Applying a template enables you to completely change the look and feel of a control, differing from styles in which you can only change predefined control properties.

To create a template:

1. Draw an object or select one from the Artboard.

2. *Do one of the following:*

   ▲ Choose Object > Edit Control Parts (Template) > Edit a Copy (**Figure 8.16**).

   ▲ Right-click the control. Choose Edit Control Parts (Template) > Edit a Copy (**Figure 8.17**).

   ▲ After selecting the control, click the name of the control in the navigation bar. From the pop-up menu, choose Edit Control Parts (Template) > Edit a Copy (**Figure 8.18**).

3. In the Create Style Resource dialog (**Figure 8.19**), enter a name for the new template.

4. Click OK to create the template.

5. Your template is now created, and Blend automatically displays the editing template mode. Changes made in this mode are applied to the newly created template. For more information about the editing template mode, see the sidebar "Editing Template Mode."

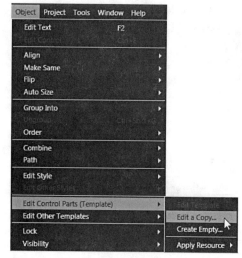

Figure 8.16 Create a new template by choosing Object > Edit Control Parts (Template) > Edit a Copy.

Figure 8.17 Create a template from the context menu of an object.

Figure 8.18 Create a template from the navigation bar.

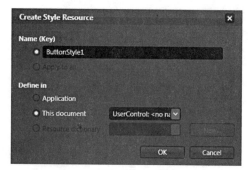

Figure 8.19 Enter a name for the template in the Create Style Resource dialog.

Editing Template Mode

Blend treats style editing and template editing in the same manner: Both the Objects and Timeline panel and the navigation bar change appearance. Also, in the editing template mode, the States panel is populated. **Figure 8.20** shows the three interface changes that occur when Blend is in the editing template mode.

The States panel shows the default states of the control. Choose a state to edit the appearance of the control in that state.

The objects in the Objects and Timeline panel are the objects that make up the control. Blend enables you to completely redefine a control's appearance by modifying these objects.

The navigation bar adds two levels in the editing template mode.

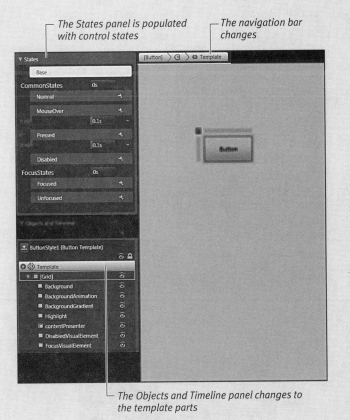

The States panel is populated with control states

The navigation bar changes

The Objects and Timeline panel changes to the template parts

Figure 8.20 Editing template mode.

To apply a template:

1. Draw an object or select one from the Artboard.

2. To apply a template to the selected object, *do one of the following:*

   ▲ Choose Object > Edit Control Parts (Template) > Apply Resource. Then, choose the template name you want to apply (**Figure 8.21**).

   Or:

   ▲ Right-click the control. Choose Edit Control Parts (Template) > Apply Resource (**Figure 8.22**).

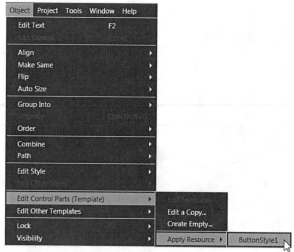

Figure 8.21 Create a new template by choosing Object > Edit Control Parts (Template) > Apply Resource.

Figure 8.22 Apply a template by right-clicking the object.

Figure 8.23 The top CheckBox control is the default look. The bottom CheckBox control uses the new template you create in this section.

Figure 8.24 Find the CheckBox in the Asset Library.

Figure 8.25 Create a copy of the CheckBox template.

Working with Templates and States

Templates enable modifications that go far beyond changing properties. The strength of defining a template is the ability to keep the existing functionality while completely redesigning a control's look. Fortunately, Blend provides the default template so that you don't have to start from scratch. This section uses the CheckBox control to illustrate how to edit the visuals and work with states. **Figure 8.23** shows the default CheckBox control and what it can look like after a template is applied to it, as you are about to do.

To change the base look:

1. In the Asset Library, select the CheckBox control (**Figure 8.24**), and draw a check box on the Artboard.

2. Create a copy of the CheckBox template by right-clicking the control and choosing Edit Control Parts (Template) > Edit a Copy (**Figure 8.25**).

Continues on next page

3. Navigate to the States panel. **Figure 8.26** shows the States panel with the Base state highlighted, indicating that changes are being made to the base state. You are now ready to change the look. On the Artboard, delete the column from the main Grid by clicking the column guide and pressing [Del] (**Figure 8.27**).

4. Move the text and the check box to look like **Figure 8.28**.

Figure 8.26 The States panel for the CheckBox control, with the Base state highlighted.

Figure 8.27 Select and delete the column from the grid.

Figure 8.28 Rearrange the control.

Figure 8.29 Move the Rectangle to the top of the Objects and Timeline panel.

Figure 8.30 The styled CheckBox.

Figure 8.31 The check mark in the base state.

Figure 8.32 Change the check mark to an X.

5. Add a Rectangle object to the control and move it to the top of the stack in the Objects and Timeline panel (**Figure 8.29**). **Figure 8.30** shows the resulting CheckBox. Remember, in Blend, topmost layers appear behind the artwork of layers located below them.

To change the checked state look:

This task extends the changes made in the previous section. First, you need to change the check mark on the base state. Then you update the opacity for the checked state.

1. In the Objects and Timeline panel, click the CheckIcon to view the outline of the check mark (**Figure 8.31**).

2. Replace the check mark with an X (**Figure 8.32**). You can achieve this task by drawing two crossing lines with the Pen tool or by using a TextBlock, typing an X character, and then converting the TextBlock to a path.

Continues on next page

WORKING WITH TEMPLATES AND STATES

3. Change the opacity for the new check mark to zero. The Opacity property is found in the Appearance section of the Properties panel (**Figure 8.33**).

4. In the States panel, click the Checked state. Notice that Blend's interface changes (**Figure 8.34**).

Figure 8.33 Change the opacity to zero.

When a state is selected, the Artboard is highlighted in red and displays the recording indicator.

The Checked state is selected

An arrow next to the CheckIcon object indicates that properties for this object are different from the base state

Figure 8.34 Blend's interface when in the Checked state.

WORKING WITH TEMPLATES AND STATES

Table 8.1

List of States

STATE NAME	STATE GROUP	DESCRIPTION
Normal	CommonStates	Default state
MouseOver	CommonStates	The pointer is over the control
Pressed	CommonStates	The control is pressed
Disabled	CommonStates	The control is disabled
Checked	CheckedStates	The control is checked
Unchecked	CheckedStates	The control is unchecked
Focused	FocusStates	The control is focused
Unfocused	FocusStates	The control does not have focus

5. In the Appearance section, change the opacity to 100% (**Figure 8.35**).

6. Finally, delete the previous check mark by selecting CheckIcon from the Objects and Timeline panel and pressing Del.

Figure 8.35 Change the opacity to 100% to show the new check mark in the Checked state.

States: A Note to Developers

States are a new feature in Silverlight 2. In fact, states were specifically developed for Silverlight 2 and are not currently implemented in WPF.

Every control template has a base set of states associated with it. States are organized into groups such as CommonStates, CheckedStates, and FocusStates. **Table 8.1** shows a list of states that can be applied to controls. Not all controls contain all of the states listed in Table 8.1. For example, a Button control does not have a CheckedStates group but a CheckBox does. The purpose of States in Blend is to enable the designer to have full control of each state a control is in as well as the transition between control states.

Note that primitive shapes, text controls, and layout control templates are not editable.

DATA AND TRIGGERS

Blend is a tool used to create rich interfaces with data and user interaction that bring life to your application. An important determination in creating a web application is choosing whether or not content and information can be updated quickly—as when manipulating the data of an external file or database—or slowly—such as updating the information and content in an authoring tool like Blend and then republishing or recompiling the entire application. In this chapter, you update content in an application by manipulating an external data source. You'll bind data sources to objects and add interactions to your interface using triggers.

Triggers are XAML-defined interactions, so you need not use another application such as Microsoft Visual Studio to write trigger code.

It's important to note that this chapter focuses on WPF applications. Silverlight 2 does not support triggers or binding directly to XML files.

Understanding Data Sources

In Blend, you can connect to two types of data sources: XML files and CLR objects. You can place the XML file in your application or on a remote server by specifying a URL. A CLR (Common Language Runtime) object is a data source created from code. (While you can programmatically create these objects, that process is beyond the scope of this book. For more information on creating a CLR object, visit www.blendsupport.com.)

To work with data in Blend, use the Data panel located below the Projects panel (**Figure 9.1**). Here you can add XML files and CLR objects, and remove data sources.

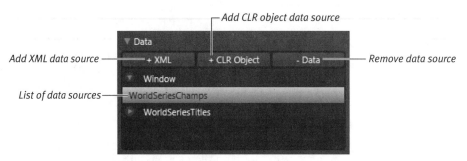

Figure 9.1 The Data panel.

Figure 9.2 The "Add new XML data source" button in the Data panel.

Figure 9.3 The Add XML Data Source dialog.

Figure 9.4 The data source is in the Data panel.

Using Data Sources

In this section, you add and remove an XML data source. You can use one of your own XML files or download a sample XML file at www.blendsupport.com/blend2vqs/files/datasources/WorldSeriesTitles.xml.

To prepare for this section, create a WPF project.

To add an XML data source:

1. In the Data panel, click the + XML (Add new XML data source) button (**Figure 9.2**).

2. In the Add XML Data Source dialog (**Figure 9.3**), enter a name for the data source in the Connection Name field. Blend uses this name to link the data source to the XML file. In the "URL for XML data" field, enter the location of the XML file. You can enter a local path or a URL. After you have entered the values, click OK.

   The newly created data source appears in the Data panel (**Figure 9.4**).

To remove a data source:

1. Select a data source you wish to delete and *do one of the following:*

   ▲ In the Data panel, click the Data (Remove data source) button (**Figure 9.5**).

   ▲ Right-click the data source to open the context menu. From the context menu, choose Remove (**Figure 9.6**).

2. In the Confirm Data Source Removal dialog (**Figure 9.7**), click Yes to delete the data source.

Figure 9.5 Click the "Remove data source" button to remove the selected data source.

Figure 9.6 Right-click the data source to open the context menu.

Figure 9.7 The Confirm Data Source Removal dialog.

Figure 9.8 Choose the ListBox control from the Asset Library.

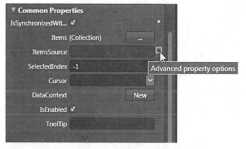

Figure 9.9 The "Advanced property options" button.

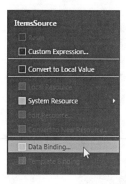

Figure 9.10 Choose Data Binding from the ItemsSource menu.

Binding Data to a ListBox

In its simplest form, data binding can link a property of a control to a data source. However, Blend has great flexibility in its data binding capabilities, allowing you to bind a wide range of properties to a data source. In this section, you bind data to the ItemsSource property of a ListBox.

To prepare for this section, create a data source from the XML file available at www.blendsupport.com/blend2vqs/files/datasources/Presidents.xml. The XML data in the file has the following structure (also called a *schema*):

```
<Presidents>

    <President>George Washington</
    → President>

    <President>John Adams</President>

    <President>Thomas Jefferson</
    → President>

</Presidents>
```

To bind data to a ListBox:

1. From the Asset Library, choose the ListBox control (**Figure 9.8**). Draw a ListBox on the Artboard.

2. In the Common Properties section of the Properties panel, click the "Advanced property options" button for the ItemsSource field (**Figure 9.9**).

3. From the ItemsSource menu, choose Data Binding (**Figure 9.10**).

Continues on next page

4. In the Create Data Binding dialog that opens, in the "Data sources" panel to the left select the data source, and in the Fields panel to the right select the elements you want to display in the control (**Figure 9.11**). After you have set up your bindings, click Finish.

5. The Artboard updates the ListBox with the bound data. **Figure 9.12** shows the resulting ListBox.

To remove a binding:

1. In the Properties panel, identify the property you want to unbind. If you're continuing with the example in the previous section, you can access the ItemsSource property in the Common Properties section (**Figure 9.13**). Click the "Advanced property options" button.

2. From the ItemsSource menu, choose Reset to unbind the data (**Figure 9.14**).

✔ Tip

■ Properties that are bound to data can be quickly identified in the Properties panel by the orange outline around the field.

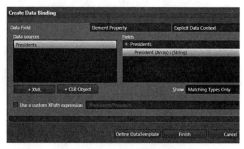

Figure 9.11 The Create Data Binding dialog.

Figure 9.12 The resulting ListBox after it has been bound with data.

Figure 9.14 Choose Reset from the ItemsSource menu.

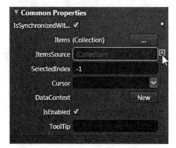

Figure 9.13 Click the "Advanced property options" button next to a data bound field.

Figure 9.15 The Triggers panel.

Understanding Triggers

In Blend, you can use triggers to add user interaction to interface elements. A trigger is a response to a specific event occurring in your application. User interactions—such as mouse movements and clicks or runtime operations such as file loading—are examples of events that can be attached to triggers. Each control in Blend has a range of events—such as MouseEnter, Click, or Loaded—that fire when the action occurs. When you create a trigger, you can listen to those events and make something happen as an action occurs. For example, when the user moves the mouse over a button, you can trigger an animated sequence for the rollover state of the button.

Silverlight 2 applications do not support triggers. The Triggers panel (**Figure 9.15**) is visible only in WPF applications.

Creating a Trigger for a Button Click

One of the most common user interactions is clicking a button. Button clicks can initiate a change to the state of your application, or perform external tasks such as opening a new web page or downloading a file. In this section, you create a trigger for a button click event.

To add a trigger:

1. Draw a button or click one on the Artboard.

2. In the Triggers panel, click the "Add event trigger" button (**Figure 9.16**).

   A default trigger is created in the Triggers panel for the Window.Loaded event, which occurs when the application window of the WPF application first loads.

3. You can change the event in the Triggers panel to one of several events available for the selected control. In this example, you use the button Click event. Start by changing the target element to the selected button by clicking the down arrow next to the object name (the default object is Window) (**Figure 9.17**).

4. In the event list, change the event to Click (**Figure 9.18**).

Figure 9.16 The "Add event trigger" button in the Triggers panel.

Figure 9.17 Change the target element type.

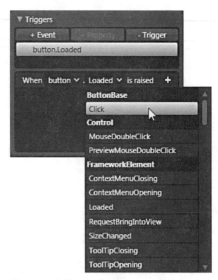

Figure 9.18 Change the event type.

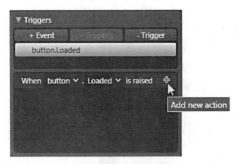

Figure 9.19 The "Add new action" button creates the trigger.

Figure 9.20 The action appears below the event.

Figure 9.21 The Storyboard Needed dialog appears if you try to add an action without a defined storyboard in your page.

5. To add an action to the trigger, click the "Add new action" button to create the action (**Figure 9.19**).

The action is added and Blend automatically enters animation mode. Now, build an animation to be displayed when the button is clicked. (See Chapter 6 for information on creating an animation.) You'll also notice that the action appears in the Triggers panel (**Figure 9.20**).

6. If a timeline does not exist in your page, the Storyboard Needed dialog appears, asking you to create one (**Figure 9.21**). Click OK to create a new timeline and enter animation mode.

To test a trigger:

After you create the trigger, test the application by *doing one of the following:*

◆ Press the F5 key.

◆ Choose Project > Test Solution (**Figure 9.22**).

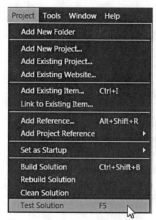

Figure 9.22 Choose Test Solution from the Project menu to test the trigger.

BUILDING A BANNER AD FOR SILVERLIGHT 2

10

As Silverlight becomes more widespread, so will the need to create Web-based advertisements using Silverlight technology. In this chapter, you'll create an example of a Silverlight-based banner ad that promotes the Blend support site, BlendSupport.com. To see a demonstration of the banner ad, visit the website at www.blendsupport.com/blend2vqs/examples/bannerad.

✔ Tip

■ While the example ad in this chapter uses text and shape graphics, you can substitute any type of artwork or media for those elements. Feel free to experiment with bitmapped graphics such as JPEG or PNG format files.

Creating the Layout

The first part of building an interactive application is to plan the layout of the user interface. In this section, you'll build a new project and size the layout for a banner ad.

To create the project:

1. Open Blend and choose New Project from the Startup menu (**Figure 10.1**), or choose File > New Project (**Figure 10.2**).

2. In the New Project dialog (**Figure 10.3**), enter the project's name in the Name field and click OK.

Figure 10.1 Choose New Project from the Startup menu.

Figure 10.2 Create a new project by choosing File > New Project.

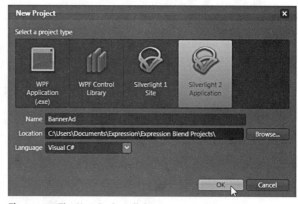

Figure 10.3 The New Project dialog.

Table 10.1

Standard Banner Ad Sizes	
TYPE OF AD	SIZE IN PIXELS
Leaderboard	728 × 90
Full banner	468 × 60
Half banner	234 × 60
Button 1	120 × 90
Button 2	120 × 60
Micro bar	88 × 31
Micro button	80 × 15
Vertical banner	120 × 240
Square button	125 × 125

Figure 10.4 The UserControl object in the Objects and Timeline panel.

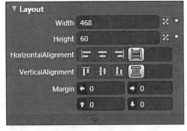

Figure 10.5 Change the Width and Height values of the UserControl object.

To change the banner size:

Web banner ads come in a variety of sizes. Most banner ad campaigns use several sizes, so you'll need to create a banner ad for each size required by the advertiser. **Table 10.1** shows the standard sizes for banner ads. The banner you'll build in this exercise uses the Full banner size, 468 by 60 pixels.

1. In the Objects and Timeline panel, click the UserControl object (**Figure 10.4**).

2. In the Layout section of the Properties panel, change the Width value to 468 and the Height value to 60 (**Figure 10.5**).

Creating the Background

After you have a correctly sized ad layout, you can start adding elements. In this section, you'll create a light ambient background with a radial gradient.

To add a gradient background:

1. In the Objects and Timeline panel, click the LayoutRoot object (**Figure 10.6**).

2. In the Brushes section of the Properties panel, choose the "Gradient brush" tab (**Figure 10.7**).

3. At the bottom of the Brushes section, click the "Radial gradient" button (**Figure 10.8**).

Figure 10.6 The LayoutRoot object in the Objects and Timeline panel.

Figure 10.7 The "Gradient brush" tab is in the Brushes section of the Properties panel.

Figure 10.8 The "Radial gradient" button is located at the bottom of the Brushes section.

Figure 10.9 Change the gradient colors.

Figure 10.10 The resulting gradient as it appears on the Artboard.

4. Change the colors in the gradient to suit your taste. **Figure 10.9** shows the use of lighter colors to create a softer tone. The effect of the gradient on the Artboard is shown in **Figure 10.10**.

5. In the Toolbox, choose the Brush Transform tool ✎ (or press G) and expand the gradient to resemble that shown in **Figure 10.11**. This effect gives the background an ambient gradient.

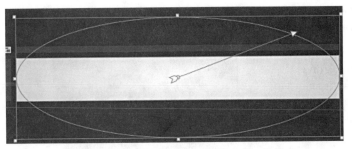

Figure 10.11 Expand the gradient using the Brush Transform tool.

To add a tag cloud to the background:

In this section, you'll add a *tag cloud* to the background. A tag cloud is a group of related words. Later in this chapter, you'll learn how to animate this tag cloud.

1. Using the TextBlock tool, [T], add text for a tag cloud to the Artboard (**Figure 10.12**). You can double-click the TextBlock tool in the Toolbox to quickly add a TextBlock to the Artboard. Create a new TextBlock for each new word.

2. Position the words on the Artboard using the Selection tool [▶] (**Figure 10.13**).

3. Change the color and text properties of each TextBlock control. You can find these properties in the Properties panel in the Brushes and Text sections, respectively (**Figure 10.14**).

Figure 10.12 TextBlocks added to the Artboard.

Figure 10.13 Position the words.

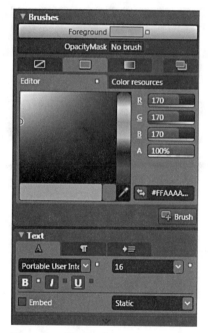

Figure 10.14 The Brushes and Text sections of the Properties panel.

Figure 10.15 Select all the TextBlocks.

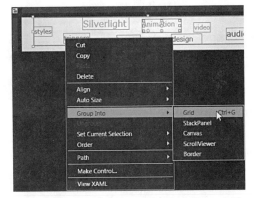

Figure 10.16 Group the selected TextBlocks into a Grid.

Figure 10.17 The banner ad with the tag cloud text added.

4. Finally, group all of the TextBlock controls into a grid by selecting the TextBlocks (**Figure 10.15**), right-clicking this selection, and choosing Group Into > Grid (**Figure 10.16**).

Figure 10.17 shows the banner ad with the tag cloud text.

✔ Tip

■ To change a property for multiple objects, select those objects and apply the property. **Figure 10.18** shows the process of selecting multiple TextBlocks and changing their Foreground colors.

Continues on next page

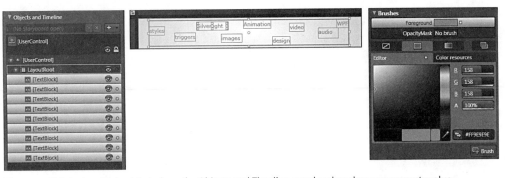

Figure 10.18 Select multiple objects from the Objects and Timeline panel and apply a new property value.

CREATING THE BACKGROUND

- If you change the font, be sure to use one of Silverlight's built-in fonts or embed the font into your application. (If you embed a font, be sure you have a redistribution license.) You can identify a built-in Silverlight font by the icon that appears to the right of the font (**Figure 10.19**).

Figure 10.19 A "Built-in Silverlight font" icon appears to the right of built-in fonts.

Figure 10.20 Add text to the Artboard.

Figure 10.21 The Text section of the Properties panel.

Creating the Main Text

After you've built the background elements for the banner ad, you're ready to create the brand identification (brand ID) for the banner ad.

To add the main text:

1. Using the TextBlock tool, add text to the Artboard (**Figure 10.20**).

2. Add emphasis to the main text. In the Text section of the Properties panel, change the text properties to size and style the text larger than the other text blocks currently on the Artboard (**Figure 10.21**).

3. Using the Selection tool, move the text to the preferred location (**Figure 10.22**).

Figure 10.22 Move the text.

To add a tag line:

1. Using the TextBlock tool, add text to the Artboard (**Figure 10.23**).

2. Using the Selection tool, resize the TextBlock (**Figure 10.24**).

3. Draw a rectangle on the Artboard to serve as the background of the tag text (**Figure 10.25**).

4. Resize the rectangle to the size of the TextBlock (**Figure 10.26**).

Figure 10.23 Add a tag line.

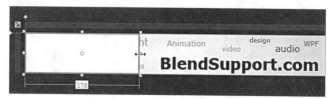

Figure 10.24 Resize the TextBlock.

Figure 10.25 Add a rectangle to become the background for the TextBlock.

Figure 10.26 Resize the rectangle.

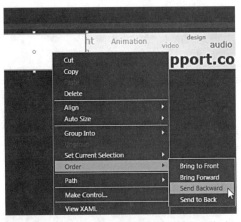

Figure 10.27 Move the rectangle behind the TextBlock.

5. Move the rectangle behind the TextBlock by right-clicking the rectangle and choosing Order > Send Backward (**Figure 10.27**).

6. Apply a gradient to the rectangle's Fill property (**Figure 10.28**). For more information on how to create a gradient, see Chapter 2.

7. Using the Brush Transform tool, rotate the gradient 90 degrees (**Figure 10.29**).

Continues on next page

Figure 10.28 Apply a gradient brush to the Fill property of the rectangle.

Figure 10.29 Rotate the gradient using the Brush Transform tool.

8. Modify the gradient colors and opacity so the background of the tag line blends into the existing banner ad's background. **Figure 10.30** shows the gradient progressing from black to a transparent black. Changing the alpha for the end color of the gradient to 0% fades the color into the background.

Figure 10.30 Modify the gradient.

9. To make the tag line text readable, choose the TextControl and change the color to white (**Figure 10.31**).

10. **Figure 10.32** shows the banner ad with all of the text and background elements included.

✔ Tip

- You can double-click the Rectangle tool in the Toolbox to quickly add a rectangle to the Artboard.

Figure 10.31 Change the text color.

Figure 10.32 The layout of the banner ad.

Adding Animation

The next step is to animate the banner ad elements; but before you begin this process, you need to assign descriptive names to each of the objects you plan to animate. If a name is not set for an object, Blend assigns a default name when that object is animated. Because the default names are not particularly descriptive, it is advisable to create an object name that will help you identify its role and its function. **Table 10.2** shows the names that were given to each object in this example.

To add a name property to an object:

1. Click an object in the Objects and Timeline panel or on the Artboard.

2. At the top of the Properties panel, enter a new name in the Name field (**Figure 10.33**).

To create the loading animation:

In this exercise, you'll create animations that start when the ad loads. First, the tag line animates in, and then the BlendSupport.com text scales and fades in from the back.

1. At the upper-right corner of the Objects and Timeline panel, click the New time-line button (**Figure 10.34**).

Table 10.2

Names for the Objects	
OBJECT	NAME
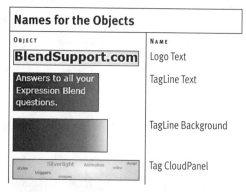	Logo Text
	TagLine Text
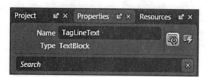	TagLine Background
	Tag CloudPanel

Figure 10.33 The Name property is located at the top of the Properties panel.

Figure 10.34 Click the New timeline button.

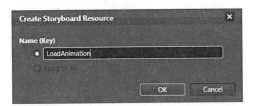

Figure 10.35 Entering the timeline name in the Create Storyboard Resource dialog.

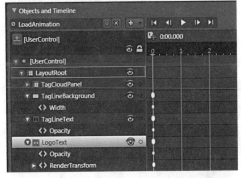

Figure 10.36 The appearance of the Artboard and the Objects and Timeline panel after the first keyframe of animation is configured.

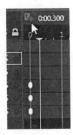

Figure 10.37 Move the playhead to 0.300 seconds.

2. In the Create Storyboard Resource dialog, enter a name for the timeline, such as *LoadAnimation,* in the Name (Key) field (**Figure 10.35**).

3. Blend automatically switches to Animation mode. As a reminder, when you work with animation, you can press F6 to switch to the Animation Workspace. For more information about Blend's Animation Workspace, see Chapter 1.

4. Create the initial state of the animation by changing the LogoText and the TagLineText to an Opacity value of 0%, the TagLineBackground's Width value to 0, and the LogoText's ScaleX and ScaleY values to 0. **Figure 10.36** shows the Artboard and the Objects and Timeline panel after these values are changed.

5. In the timeline, move the playhead to 0.300 seconds (**Figure 10.37**).

Continues on next page

6. Change the Width value of the TagLineBackground to 180 (**Figure 10.38**).

7. Select the TagLineText object and click the Record Keyframe button (**Figure 10.39**). See Chapter 6 for more information about keyframes.

8. In the timeline, move the playhead to 0.700 seconds (**Figure 10.40**).

Figure 10.38 Change the width of the TagLineBackground.

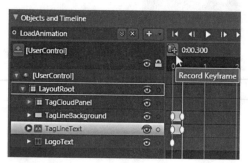

Figure 10.39 The Record Keyframe button.

Figure 10.40 Move the playhead to 0.700 seconds.

9. Change the Opacity value for the TagLineText to 100 (**Figure 10.41**).

10. Choose the LogoText object and click the Record Keyframe button (**Figure 10.42**).

11. In the timeline, move the playhead to 01.000 second (**Figure 10.43**).

Figure 10.41 Change the Opacity value of the TagLineText to 100.

Figure 10.42 The Record Keyframe button.

Figure 10.43 Move the playhead to 01.000 second.

12. Select the LogoText object and change the opacity value from 0% to 100% and the ScaleX and ScaleY values to 1 (**Figure 10.44**).

13. In the Objects and Timeline panel, click the Play button to preview the animation (**Figure 10.45**).

Figure 10.44 Change the Opacity and the Scale values for the LogoText object.

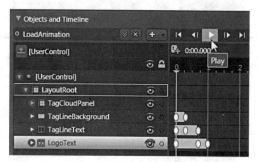

Figure 10.45 Play the timeline.

Figure 10.46 Click the New timeline button.

Figure 10.47 The Create Storyboard Resource dialog with a timeline name entered.

To create an ambient tag cloud animation:

At the beginning of this chapter, you created a group of words, or a tag cloud, in the background. This exercise adds motion to that tag cloud. In a banner ad, it's important to visually grab the user's attention. One way to achieve this without annoying the user is to add ambient motion.

1. At the upper-right corner of the Objects and Timeline panel, click the New timeline button (**Figure 10.46**).

2. In the Create Storyboard Resource dialog, enter a name for the timeline, such as AmbientBackgroundAnimation, in the Name (Key) field (**Figure 10.47**).

3. Because this animation will move slowly, you'll want to adjust the timeline to show a greater amount of time. At the bottom of the timeline, drag the "Timeline zoom" slider to the left to zoom out (**Figure 10.48**) until you can see a minute of events in the timeline. When dragging, your mouse pointer will disappear. Blend locks the mouse when you zoom using the Timeline zoom slider.

Continues on next page

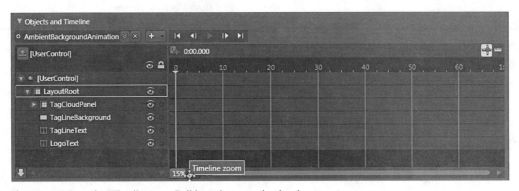

Figure 10.48 Drag the "Timeline zoom" slider to increase the time increments.

ADDING ANIMATION

4. In the Objects and Timeline panel, choose the TagCloudPanel and click the Record Keyframe button (**Figure 10.49**).

5. Move the playhead to 30 seconds (**Figure 10.50**).

6. Move the TagCloudPanel to the left, near the position shown in **Figure 10.51**.

7. Move the playhead to 60 seconds (**Figure 10.52**).

8. Reposition the TagCloudPanel near the location shown in **Figure 10.53**.

Figure 10.49 Record a keyframe at 00.000 seconds.

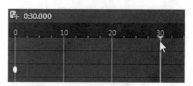

Figure 10.50 Move the playhead to 30 seconds.

Figure 10.51 Move the TagCloudPanel for the 30 second keyframe.

Figure 10.52 Move the playhead to 60 seconds.

Figure 10.53 Move the TagCloudPanel for the 60 second keyframe.

Figure 10.54 Select the timeline.

Figure 10.55 Change the properties of the timeline.

9. Now you need to configure the animation to loop automatically during playback. In the Objects and Timeline panel, click the animation name (**Figure 10.54**).

10. In the Common Properties section of the Properties panel, select AutoReverse and change the RepeatBehavior value to Forever (**Figure 10.55**).

11. Click the Play button to preview the animation (**Figure 10.56**). Notice the slow movement of the tag cloud. This movement provides a subtle effect intended to capture the attention of users.

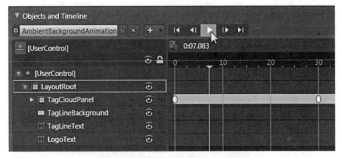

Figure 10.56 Click the Play button to preview the animation.

ADDING ANIMATION

To add easing to an animation:

The effect of *easing* a transition adds polish to your animation. Instead of presenting a flat, linear animation, you can add a sense of acceleration or deceleration to make the motion feel less programmed and more natural.

1. In the Objects and Timeline panel, open the LoadAnimation timeline by clicking the down arrow button next to the box labeled "(No storyboard open)" (**Figure 10.57**).

2. Select the 0.3 second keyframe for the TagLineBackground object (**Figure 10.58**).

3. In the Properties panel, change the x, y values to those shown in **Figure 10.59**. See Chapter 6 for more information about easing keyframes.

4. Select the 01.000 second keyframe for the LogoText object (**Figure 10.60**) and apply the easing as you did in step 3.

5. Click the Play button to view the animation. Notice that the background and the logo ease in, making their motion appear more natural.

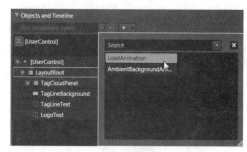

Figure 10.57 Open the LoadAnimation timeline.

Figure 10.58 Select the last keyframe for the TagLineBackground object.

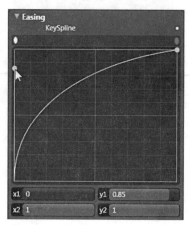

Figure 10.59 Add easing to the keyframe.

Figure 10.60 Select the last keyframe for the LogoText object.

Adding Interactivity

Finally, you need to initiate the animations in code, as well as add a click handler to the banner ad. The code is kept in a separate file, known as the *code-behind file*. Its purpose is to clearly separate the user interface from the code. For more information, see "What Is a Code-Behind File?" in Chapter 1.

To initiate animations:

1. From the Project panel, open the Page.xaml.cs file.

2. Add this code to the Page constructor (line 16 in **Figure 10.61**):

   this.Loaded += new
   → RoutedEventHandler(Page_Loaded);

   This code registers the Loaded event for the control.

Continues on next page

```
1 using System;
2 using System.Windows;
3 using System.Windows.Controls;
4 using System.Windows.Browser;
5 using System.Windows.Input;
6
7 namespace BannerAd
8 {
9     public partial class Page : UserControl
10    {
11        public Page()
12        {
13            InitializeComponent();
14
15            //Register the Loaded event.
16            this.Loaded += new RoutedEventHandler(Page_Loaded);
17
18            //Register the MouseLeftButtonUp event
19            this.MouseLeftButtonUp += new MouseButtonEventHandler(Page_MouseLeftButtonUp)
20
21            // Set the cursor for the Banner Ad.
22            this.Cursor = Cursors.Hand;
23        }
24
25        /// <summary>
26        /// Fires after the page finishes render the controls.
27        /// </summary>
28        void Page_Loaded(object sender, RoutedEventArgs e)
29        {
30            this.LoadAnimation.Begin();
31            this.AmbientBackgroundAnimation.Begin();
32        }
33
34        /// <summary>
35        /// Fires when the user releases the mouse left button.
36        /// </summary>
37        void Page_MouseLeftButtonUp(object sender, MouseButtonEventArgs e)
38        {
39            HtmlPage.Window.Navigate(new Uri("http://www.blendsupport.com"), "_target");
40        }
41    }
42 }
```

Figure 10.61 The code in Page.xaml.cs.

3. Add the following method to the class:

```
void Page_Loaded(object sender,
→ RoutedEventArgs e)
{
  this.LoadAnimation.Begin();
  this.AmbientBackgroundAnimation.
  → Begin();
}
```

This method calls the Begin event on the timelines created in Blend.

To add click functionality:

1. In the Page.xaml.cs file, add this code to the constructor:

```
this.MouseLeftButtonUp += new
→ MouseButtonEventHandler(Page_
→ MouseLeftButtonUp);
```

This code registers the `MouseLeftButtonUp` event for the control that detects when the user clicks the banner ad. Using the `MouseLeftButtonUp` event instead of the `MouseLeftButtonDown` event is the preferred click behavior for a link or a button in HTML. By only enabling the `MouseLeftButtonUp` event, the user can cancel the action of clicking down on the ad by rolling off the ad and releasing the left mouse button.

2. Add this directive to the top of the file:

```
using System.Windows.Browser;
```

You will need this library to change the URL.

3. Finally, add the handler that was registered in step 1:

```
void Page_MouseLeftButtonUp(object
→ sender, MouseButtonEventArgs e)
{
    HtmlPage.Window.Navigate(new
    → Uri("http://www.blendsupport.com"),
    → "_target");
}
```

In this handler, you direct the browser to a new destination URL, www.blendsupport.com. Use the HtmlPage.Window.Navigate method to change the URL.

Continues on next page

4. After you write the code, press ⌊F5⌋ in Blend to run the banner ad. **Figure 10.62** shows the banner ad playing in the context of a web browser.

✔ Tip

■ Because Silverlight applications are web based, it's a good habit to change the cursor to the standard hand icon 🖐 for clickable objects. Like most properties, you can set the Cursor property in both XAML and in the code-behind. Line 22 of Figure 10.61 sets the Cursor for the banner ad to a hand.

Figure 10.62 The banner ad running in a browser.

CREATING A VIDEO PLAYER IN SILVERLIGHT

One of the most exciting aspects of Silverlight is the video experience, and you can use Blend to increase the interactivity and involvement of that experience. In 2008, Silverlight was the technology chosen to showcase hundreds of video streams, including footage of the Beijing Olympic Games and events surrounding the Democratic National Convention. In this chapter, you'll use your accumulated Blend and Silverlight knowledge to create a custom-styled Silverlight 2 video player and later expand the way you integrate video content on the Web.

Creating the Layout

Choosing layout controls for your video player is an important first step when building a video experience. The layout controls dictate whether the user interface (UI) will be scalable or fixed. A scalable UI reflows the playback controls under the video playback area as you resize the application window, whereas a fixed UI has a stationary controls and video playback area.

To create the project:

1. Open Blend and, from the Startup menu, choose New Project (**Figure 11.1**), or choose File > New Project (**Figure 11.2**).

2. In the New Project dialog (**Figure 11.3**), enter a value in the Name field, choose the location, and click OK.

Figure 11.1 Choose New Project from the Startup menu.

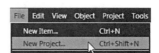

Figure 11.2 Create a new project by choosing File > New Project.

Figure 11.3 The New Project dialog.

Figure 11.4 Click UserControl in the Objects and Timeline panel.

Figure 11.5 Change the width and height for the control.

3. When the project opens, change the width and height values to your desired size. Click UserControl in the Objects and Timeline panel (**Figure 11.4**), and in the Layout section of the Properties panel, enter new values in the Width and Height fields (**Figure 11.5**).

The size for this example, 400 × 255 pixels, was dictated by the size of the high definition (HD) video and its 16:9 aspect ratio. The original dimensions of the HD video, 1920 × 1080 pixels, were scaled down to 400 × 255 pixels to achieve a more Internet-friendly file size for the deployed video. An extra 30 pixels are added to the height of the video frame to accommodate the video controls located below the video playback area.

Continues on next page

CREATING THE LAYOUT

4. Next, create a row in the LayoutRoot grid to hold the video controls. First, from the Objects and Timeline panel, select the LayoutRoot. Then, click the blue ruler to the left of the LayoutRoot on the Artboard (**Figure 11.6**).

Because this example allocates 30 pixels for the video controls, you need to ensure that the row is 30 pixels in height. Click the newly created row arrow on the Artboard (**Figure 11.7**); then set the height for the row in the Properties panel by entering a new value in the Height field (**Figure 11.8**). The pop-up menu displays the type of units that can be used to define the row height. Choose Pixel to assign an absolute value to the height.

Figure 11.6 Create a new row for the LayoutRoot by clicking the left ruler.

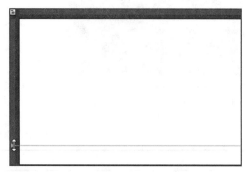

Figure 11.7 Select the row to display its properties in the Layout panel.

Figure 11.8 Set the height for the selected row.

CREATING THE LAYOUT

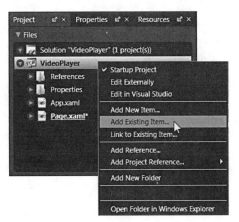

Figure 11.9 The context menu for the project.

Importing the Video

In this section, you'll add a video to the project and place the video into the top row of the LayoutRoot grid. You can download a sample Windows Media Video file at www.blendsupport.com/blend2vqs/files/media.

To add a video:

1. In the Project panel, right-click the name of the project and choose Add Existing Item (**Figure 11.9**). You could also choose Link to Existing Item, which would link the media to the project file instead of importing the video file into the project. For more information about using the Link to Existing Item option, see Chapter 7.

2. In the Add Existing Item dialog, navigate to the video you want to import, select it, and click Open (**Figure 11.10**).

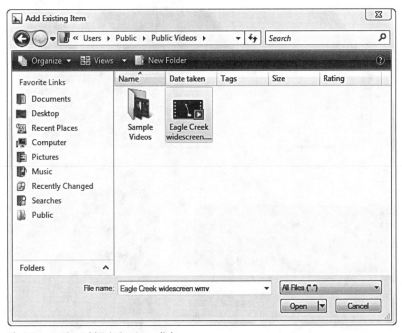

Figure 11.10 The Add Existing Item dialog.

3. Add the video to the project by dragging the video from the Project panel to the Artboard (**Figure 11.11**). When the video is added to the Artboard, a MediaElement control is automatically created that sets the source property to the video content. An alternative way to add video to the project is to select the MediaElement control from the Asset Library in the Toolbox. For more information about this procedure, see Chapter 7.

4. You need to modify the MediaElement control to size the video to fit correctly in the first row, as shown in **Figure 11.12**. In the Layout section of the Properties panel, change the value for Margin to 0 and change RowSpan to a value of 1 (**Figure 11.13**).

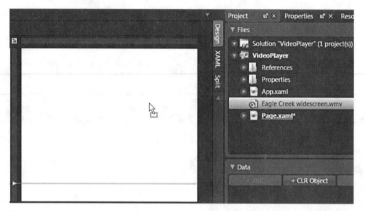

Figure 11.11 Drag the video from the Project panel to the Artboard.

Figure 11.12 The video is in the top row.

Figure 11.13 The layout properties for the MediaElement control.

Figure 11.14 Choose the StackPanel from the Toolbox.

Figure 11.15 The default StackPanel is added to the top left of the Artboard.

Figure 11.16 The layout properties of the StackPanel.

Figure 11.17 The StackPanel in the second row of the LayoutRoot grid.

Adding the Video Controls

Now that the video has been added to the interface, you can add playback controls to the Artboard. In this section, you add controls for playing, pausing, and scrubbing the video, along with controls to mute and control the volume level and to enable full-screen playback.

To add the controls container:

While you could add the controls directly to the second row of the LayoutRoot, a better way to manage the layout of the controls is to use a StackPanel. Without a StackPanel, you would need to set absolute margins for the controls. With a StackPanel, the horizontal positioning of the controls occurs automatically.

1. From the Toolbox, choose the StackPanel (**Figure 11.14**).

2. Double-click the StackPanel icon 📇 to add a default 100 × 100–pixel StackPanel to the Artboard. **Figure 11.15** shows the default StackPanel added to the Artboard.

3. Because the StackPanel is the container for the video playback controls, it needs to be moved to the second row. In the Layout section of the Properties panel, change the Row value from 0 to 1. Also, change the Width and Height values from 100 to Auto, HorizontalAlignment and VerticalAlignment to Stretch, and Orientation to Horizontal. **Figure 11.16** shows the Layout section of the Properties panel with the correct properties. **Figure 11.17** shows the Artboard after these changes have been made.

To add video controls:

Now you're ready to add the video playback controls to the newly created StackPanel.

1. On the Artboard, double-click the StackPanel. A yellow selection outline appears to indicate that it is the active panel (**Figure 11.18**).

2. The play and pause functions will be different states of the same button. Unlike a regular Button control, a ToggleButton control can automatically manage two different states. In the Asset Library, select the ToggleButton (**Figure 11.19**) and add it to the Artboard (**Figure 11.20**).

3. To add the scrubber control, in the Asset Library, find the Slider control and add it to the Artboard (**Figure 11.21**).

Figure 11.18 The StackPanel has a yellow outline after the control is double-clicked.

Figure 11.19 Click the ToggleButton in the Asset Library.

Figure 11.20 The ToggleButton added to the StackPanel.

Figure 11.21 The Slider is added, and will be used as the scrubber.

Figure 11.22 The ToggleButton can be found in the Toolbox, since it was recently used.

Figure 11.23 The mute ToggleButton added.

Figure 11.24 The video player with the controls added.

4. The process of adding a mute button is the same as adding a play/pause button. However, because you have already used the ToggleButton control, you do not need to access the Asset Library. Instead, you can click and hold the mouse button over the Slider icon in the Toolbox to display the ToggleButton in the submenu (**Figure 11.22**). **Figure 11.23** shows the second ToggleButton control added to the Artboard.

5. To add a volume control, repeat the procedure in step 3 to add a Slider.

6. To add the full-screen toggle, add a ToggleButton using the procedure described in step 2.

7. After you have added the controls, the player should resemble **Figure 11.24**.

Styling the Play Button

After you've added the controls, you should style them to look like video controls. The play/pause button is a ToggleButton control with two states. This exercise shows how to build the two states into one control.

To make the play state:

1. In the StackPanel, right-click the first ToggleButton control and choose Edit Control Parts (Template) > Edit a Copy (**Figure 11.25**) to create a new style.

2. Give the new style a name, such as PlayPauseButtonStyle, by entering it in the Name (Key) field. Click OK (**Figure 11.26**).

3. You are now editing the template of the ToggleButton control. Draw a triangle to represent the play icon. (For information on drawing a triangle, see Chapter 3.) **Figure 11.27** shows the triangle in the template and its associated layout properties.

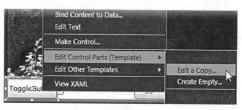

Figure 11.25 Create a new style.

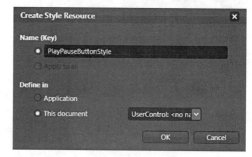

Figure 11.26 In the Create Style Resource dialog, enter a name for the new style.

Figure 11.27 The triangle is added to the template. The right image shows the properties of the triangle.

STYLING THE PLAY BUTTON

Figure 11.28 The fill has a gradient. Click the Convert brush to resource button to make it a resource.

Figure 11.29 Delete contentPresenter from the template.

Figure 11.30 The top image is the control before the contentPresenter is deleted; the bottom image shows the ToggleButton after the deletion.

4. As you did in Lesson 10, add a gradient as the fill and convert the Brush to a resource (**Figure 11.28**). This gradient will be used later in the other controls.

5. Delete the default ToggleButton text in the ToggleButton control. In the Objects and Timeline panel, choose the contentPresenter layer (**Figure 11.29**) and press Del. **Figure 11.30** shows the button before and after the deletion of the contentPresenter layer.

To make a pause icon:

Now that you've added the play icon, you're ready to create the pause icon. You complete this task by adding the icon to the control and toggling its visibility during the Checked state.

1. Create the pause icon by drawing two parallel rectangles (**Figure 11.31**).

2. To make the pause icon appear consistent with the play icon, change the rectangles' fill to the gradient resource that you previously created. In Blend, you can perform a multiple selection and change the fill. **Figure 11.32** shows both rectangles selected and the Fill changed to the gradient resource.

3. Encapsulate both rectangles into their own Grid control by right-clicking the selected rectangles and choosing Group Into > Grid from the context menu (**Figure 11.33**).

4. Adjust the rectangles' positions by double-clicking the newly created Grid and moving the rectangles (**Figure 11.34**).

Figure 11.31 Two parallel rectangles represent the pause icon.

Figure 11.32 Use the gradient resource for the Fill of the pause icon.

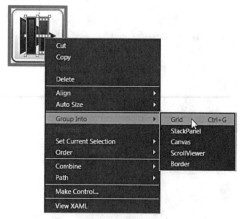

Figure 11.33 Group the pause icon into a Grid.

Figure 11.34 Reposition the rectangles after grouping into a Grid.

STYLING THE PLAY BUTTON

Figure 11.35 The Base state is selected in the States panel.

Figure 11.36 Change the Opacity for the pause grid to 0% in the Base state.

Figure 11.37 Change CheckStates to Checked.

To set the state of the button:

Now that both the play and pause icons are created, you need to change the visibility of the icons for each state of the ToggleButton control. In this section, you will work with states. For more information, refer to "Working with Templates and States" in Chapter 8.

1. Open the States panel to view the current active state, the Base state (**Figure 11.35**). The play and pause icons are both visible in this Base state. However, you want the pause icon visible and the play icon hidden when the user clicks the ToggleButton. To add this behavior, in the Appearance section of the Properties panel, locate the Opacity data field for the Grid control that contains the pause rectangles. Change the Opacity value to 0% (**Figure 11.36**).

2. In the States panel, click the Checked state (**Figure 11.37**). A red outline appears around the Artboard to indicate that all changes made in this mode will apply to the Checked state.

3. Select the pause grid. Change the Opacity value for the pause icon to 100 and the Opacity value for the play icon to 0. **Figure 11.38** shows the appearance of the pause icon when it is visible on the Artboard. Also, in the Objects and Timeline panel, a red arrow is now displayed next to the objects that have changed properties for the selected state (**Figure 11.39**).

4. To test the modified states, press F5 and click the button. This opens the application in a new web browser.

Figure 11.38 The pause icon is visible in the Checked state.

Figure 11.39 Red arrows appear next to objects that have changed properties for the selected state.

STYLING THE PLAY BUTTON

Figure 11.40 Select the default objects from the copied template in the Objects and Timeline panel.

To clean up the control:

Optionally, you can remove unnecessary objects from the PlayPauseButtonStyle. It's considered a best practice to keep only those elements that are needed to achieve the desired look and feel of the style.

1. In the States panel, click the Base state.

2. In the Objects and Timeline panel, select all the objects that Blend automatically created (**Figure 11.40**).

3. Press Del. A warning message is displayed to let you know that some of the states have been changed (**Figure 11.41**). Don't worry about this warning—Blend has deleted the references. **Figure 11.42** shows the modified control.

✔ Tip

■ To provide a more Web-friendly experience when using clickable controls such as a ToggleButton, assign the Hand cursor in the Common Properties section of the Properties panel (**Figure 11.43**). The presence of the Hand cursor more clearly informs users that an object may be clicked.

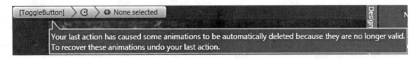

Figure 11.41 The warning indicates that Blend has deleted objects referenced in previous states.

Figure 11.42 The final control.

Figure 11.43 The Cursor field in the Common Properties section of the Properties panel.

Styling the Volume Button

The volume button requires graphics to display the muted and unmuted states of the video. The process for styling this button is just like styling the play/pause button. You create a copy of the template and edit the checked state.

To create the default state:

1. In the StackPanel, right-click the middle ToggleButton control and choose Edit Controls Parts (Template) > Edit a Copy (**Figure 11.44**).

2. In the Create Style Resource dialog, enter a new name for the style, such as MuteButtonStyle, and click OK (**Figure 11.45**).

3. You are now editing the template of the mute button. In the default state, create a mute icon by drawing two rectangles side by side, as shown in **Figure 11.46**.

4. Next, right-click the rightmost rectangle and choose Path > Convert to Path to convert the rectangle to a path (**Figure 11.47**).

Figure 11.44 Create a new style for the volume ToggleButton.

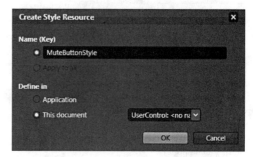

Figure 11.45 In the Create Style Resource dialog, enter a name for the new style.

Figure 11.46 Draw two rectangles side by side to represent the speaker in your mute icon.

Figure 11.47 Convert the right rectangle to a Path using the context menu.

STYLING THE VOLUME BUTTON

Figure 11.48 With the Direct Selection tool, move the nodes to have the rectangle look like a speaker.

Figure 11.49 Draw three lines to represent sound waves coming out of the speaker.

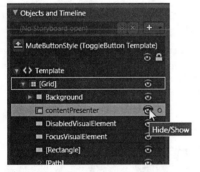

Figure 11.50 Hide an object by clicking the eye icon next to it in the Objects and Timeline panel.

Figure 11.51 The speaker icon with the contentPresenter object hidden.

5. Using the Direct Selection tool, move the nodes of the rectangle to suggest a speaker shape (**Figure 11.48**).

6. Use the Line tool to draw three parallel lines representing sound waves (**Figure 11.49**). You'll notice that it's difficult to see the newly drawn lines because the default label text, ToggleButton, appears behind the artwork. To hide the word *ToggleButton,* in the Objects and Timeline panel, click the eye (Hide/Show) icon next to the contentPresenter layer (**Figure 11.50**). The label text is hidden, and you can more easily view the drawn lines (**Figure 11.51**).

Continues on next page

STYLING THE VOLUME BUTTON

7. To vertically center the lines with one another, select all three lines, right-click them, and choose Align > Vertical Centers (**Figure 11.52**).

8. Using the Direct Selection tool, you can curve the sound wave lines to more clearly suggest sound waves (**Figure 11.53**). Select a line, hold down Alt, and drag the lines.

   Reposition the sound waves as you see fit. **Figure 11.54** moves them closer to the speaker to make a tighter icon.

9. Apply the gradient that you previously created. Select the two objects that make up the speaker icon, and from the Brushes section of the Properties panel, apply the gradient (**Figure 11.55**).

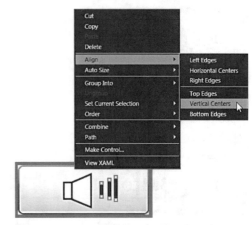

Figure 11.52 Align vertical centers using the context menu.

Figure 11.53 Curve the sound waves by holding down the Alt key and dragging the lines.

Figure 11.54 Move the sound waves closer to the speaker.

Figure 11.55 Apply the gradient resource to the speaker icon.

Figure 11.56 Draw a diagonal line to indicate that the volume is muted.

To add the muted indicator:

1. Draw a diagonal line over the speaker to indicate that the volume is muted (**Figure 11.56**).

2. Change the thickness of the line to make it more prominent. In the Appearance section of the Properties panel, change the StrokeThickness value to the desired line thickness (**Figure 11.57**).

Figure 11.57 Increase the StrokeThickness value to make the line more prominent.

To enable the state of the mute button:

1. Change the Opacity value of the diagonal line from 100% to 0% (**Figure 11.58**).

2. In the States panel, click the Checked state (**Figure 11.59**).

3. In the Checked state, change the Opacity value of the diagonal line to 100% and the Opacity value of the objects in the sound wave to 0% (**Figure 11.60**).

4. To test the states, press F5 to open the application. Once the application is loaded, click the mute button.

Figure 11.58 Change the Opacity value of the diagonal line in the Base state.

Figure 11.59 Change CheckStates to Checked.

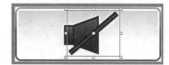

Figure 11.60 The icon in the checked state.

STYLING THE VOLUME BUTTON

Figure 11.61 Select the default objects from the copied template in the Objects and Timeline panel.

Figure 11.62 The final mute button control.

To clean up the button:

Just as you did when cleaning up the play/pause ToggleButton, you can optionally remove elements that are not required for the mute button states. For the sake of a clean design, this section outlines the steps to remove the default objects, leaving only the speaker icon.

1. In the States panel, choose the Base state.

2. In the Objects and Timeline panel, select all the objects that Blend created as part of the default template, as shown in **Figure 11.61**.

3. Press Del. **Figure 11.62** shows the cleaned version of the ToggleButton control for the mute button.

Styling the Full-Screen Button

To style the last ToggleButton control for the full-screen button, you'll repeat the process you used for the two previous ToggleButton controls. For brevity's sake, this exercise assumes that you have converted the button to a style resource.

To create the full-screen button:

1. Create an icon in the Base state that resembles **Figure 11.63**. Create two rectangles with gradient fills, and draw the arrow using the Line tool.

2. In the States panel, choose the Checked state, resize the inner rectangle, and rotate the arrow to point to the lower-right corner, as in **Figure 11.64**.

Figure 11.63 The full-screen button in the Base state.

Figure 11.64 The full-screen button in the Checked state.

Figure 11.65 Create a new style for the video scrubber slider.

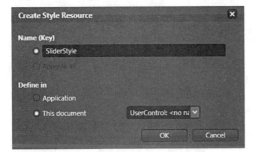

Figure 11.66 In the Create Style Resource dialog, enter a name for the new style.

Figure 11.67 Select the HorizontalThumb layer from the Objects and Timeline panel.

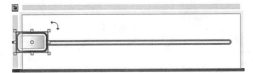

Figure 11.68 Rotate the HorizontalThumb 90 degrees on the Artboard.

Styling the Scrubber and the Volume Slider

In this section, you create a unique style for the scrubber and volume slider by creating a style for the scrubber, and then applying that style to the volume slider.

To create the scrubber style:

1. In the StackPanel, right-click the first Slider control and choose Edit Control Parts (Template) > Edit a Copy (**Figure 11.65**).

2. In the Name (Key) field of the Create Style Resource dialog, enter a new name for the style, such as *SliderStyle,* and click OK (**Figure 11.66**).

3. You are now editing the template. First, you will rotate the horizontal thumb 90 degrees. In the Objects and Timeline panel, expand the HorizontalTemplate and select the HorizontalThumb layer (**Figure 11.67**).

4. On the Artboard, rotate the HorizontalThumb 90 degrees to resemble **Figure 11.68**.

Continues on next page

5. Change the background of the HorizonalThumb to match the play/pause ToggleButton and the mute ToggleButton.

Right-click the HorizontalThumb, and choose Edit Control Parts (Template) > Edit a Copy (**Figure 11.69**).

6. In the Create Style Resource dialog, enter a name for the new style (**Figure 11.70**).

7. Expand the Background > Grid group in the Objects and Timeline panel and click the BackgroundGradient layer (**Figure 11.71**).

8. Change the fill by selecting the Brush resources tab in the Brushes section of the Properties panel (**Figure 11.72**).

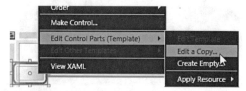

Figure 11.69 Create a copy of the template for the HorizontalThumb.

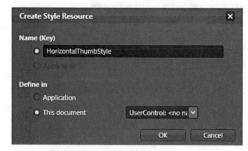

Figure 11.70 Name the style.

Figure 11.71 Select BackgroundGradient from the Objects and Timeline panel.

Figure 11.72 Change the Fill to the brush resource.

STYLING THE SCRUBBER AND THE VOLUME SLIDER

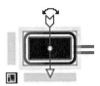

Figure 11.73 Use the Brush Transform tool to rotate the gradient.

9. Using the Brush Transform tool from the Toolbox, rotate the gradient 90 degrees (**Figure 11.73**).

10. Finally, expand the width of the Slider track from 3 pixels to 5 pixels.

   At the top of the Artboard, click the HorizontalThumb in the Navigation bar (**Figure 11.74**).

11. In the Objects and Timeline panel, select the TrackRectangle layer (**Figure 11.75**).

12. In the Layout section of the Properties panel, change the Height value to 5 (**Figure 11.76**).

Figure 11.74 Navigate back to the Slider template.

Figure 11.75 Select TrackRectangle in the Objects and Timeline panel.

Figure 11.76 The track is now 5 pixels tall.

To apply the style to the volume slider:

This section uses the previous section's Slider style and applies it to the volume slider.

Figure 11.77 Select the volume slider.

1. Select the volume slider, the rightmost object in the video controls (**Figure 11.77**).

2. In the Miscellaneous section of the Properties panel, click the "Advanced property options" button for the Style property (**Figure 11.78**).

Figure 11.78 The "Advanced property options" button.

3. From the "Advanced property options" menu, choose Local Resource > SliderStyle (**Figure 11.79**).

4. When the style is applied, a green outline appears around the value of the style property (**Figure 11.80**).

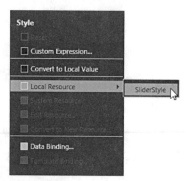

Figure 11.79 Apply the SliderStyle to the volume slider.

Figure 11.80 The styled volume slider with a green outline.

Table 11.1

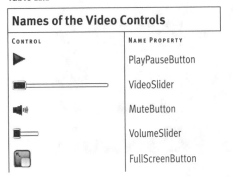

Names of the Video Controls	
CONTROL	NAME PROPERTY
▶	PlayPauseButton
▬▭	VideoSlider
🔊	MuteButton
▮▬	VolumeSlider
🔲	FullScreenButton

Figure 11.81 The complete video player UI.

Figure 11.82 The Name property appears at the top of the Properties panel.

Adding Interactivity

When you test the program, the video scrubber does not update, the mute button does not affect the sound, and clicking the full-screen button does not perform an action. Building the UI is just the first half of the task. You now have to tie the elements to the video control to create the proper responses (**Figure 11.81**). It's time to add interaction by modifying the code.

To prepare the objects in Blend to be consumed from the code-behind, give a name to all the objects. The Name property is the top property in the Properties panel (**Figure 11.82**). **Table 11.1** shows how each control should be named.

Modifying the code

In the Project panel, locate the Page.xaml.cs file (**Figure 11.83**). This file contains the code that makes everything work in your application. Download the code from www.blendsupport. com/blend2vqs/files/videoplayer/Page.xaml. cs.zip and add it to the page. The code in this file wires up the controls to the respective functionality.

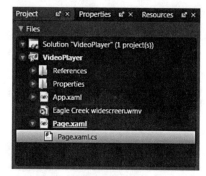

Figure 11.83 The Page.xaml.cs file is found in the Project panel under Page.xaml.

BROWSING DESKTOP IMAGES WITH WPF

12

One of the exciting features of a WPF application is its ability to interact directly with the desktop. Silverlight applications have limited access to local resources, but WPF applications can read and write files to a user's computer. In this chapter, you'll build an image browser as a WPF application.

Creating the Layout

The image browser built in this chapter is shown in **Figure 12.1**. It allows you to pick a folder (or directory) on your local system and view any images there.

To set up the project:

1. Open Blend and choose New Project from the Startup menu (**Figure 12.2**), or choose File > New Project (**Figure 12.3**).

Figure 12.1 The final image browser.

Figure 12.2 Choose New Project from the Startup menu.

Figure 12.3 Create a new project by choosing File > New Project.

2. In the New Project dialog, click WPF Application (.exe). In the Name field, enter ImageViewer (**Figure 12.4**). Click OK.

3. Change the size of the default Window from the default size of 640 × 480 pixels. It is convenient to work with a smaller Window during this initial phase. **Figure 12.5** shows the Window resized to 500 × 400 pixels.

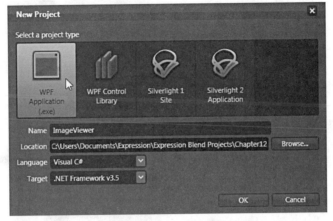

Figure 12.4 The New Project dialog.

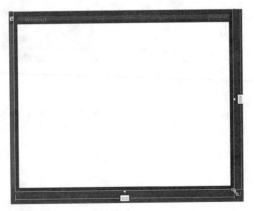

Figure 12.5 Resize the Window.

To create the browser layout:

Three areas of interest exist in the layout of this application:

◆ The folder location at the top of the application

◆ The list of images to the left

◆ The selected image to the right

These three areas logically can be broken up into panels. The top panel easily lends itself to a DockPanel control, and the left and main image viewing area can stretch itself to the size of the grid column.

1. In the LayoutRoot, create two columns and two rows. The top row includes the folder location, the left column contains the list of images, and the right column displays the selected image. To create a column, click the blue ruler at the top of the Artboard to create the columns (**Figure 12.6**). Click the left ruler to create the rows (**Figure 12.7**).

2. The container for the folder location is DockPanel. To add a DockPanel to the top of the Window, in the Toolbox, position your mouse pointer over the Grid tool and click and hold down the mouse button to open the layout fly-out menu. From the menu, choose the DockPanel (**Figure 12.8**). Double-click the DockPanel icon in the Toolbox to add a DockPanel with a default size to the Artboard (**Figure 12.9**).

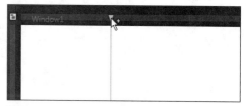

Figure 12.6 Click the blue ruler at the top of the Artboard to divide the LayoutRoot into two columns.

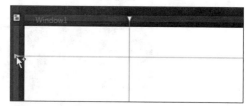

Figure 12.7 Click the blue ruler to the left of the Artboard to divide the LayoutRoot into two rows.

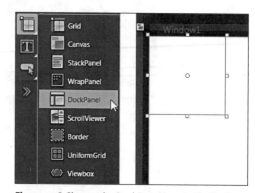

Figure 12.8 Choose the DockPanel icon in the Toolbox.

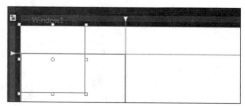

Figure 12.9 The default DockPanel added to the Artboard.

Figure 12.10 The layout properties for the DockPanel.

Figure 12.11 The DockPanel at the top of the Window.

Figure 12.12 Choose the ListBox control from the Toolbox.

3. When the DockPanel is added by double-clicking the icon in the Toolbox, you need to adjust a few properties to place the DockPanel in the top row. In the Layout section of the Properties panel, change the values as indicated in **Figure 12.10**. After changing the values, your Artboard should resemble **Figure 12.11**.

4. Now that the container for the folder has been added, it's time to add a container for the list of images. Start by adding a ListBox to the first column of the second row. In the Toolbox, from the Asset tools fly-out menu, choose ListBox (**Figure 12.12**).

Continues on next page

CREATING THE LAYOUT

5. Double-click the ListBox icon in the Toolbox to add a ListBox control to the Artboard (**Figure 12.13**).

6. As you did in step 3, you will need to change a few properties to ensure that the ListBox is in the correct layout. Change the properties for the ListBox to match **Figure 12.14** .

7. Finally, add an Image to the second row and second column, the main image area of the application. When the user chooses an image from the leftmost ListBox, the larger version of that image appears in this Image control. To add the Image control, search for *image* in the Asset Library (**Figure 12.15**).

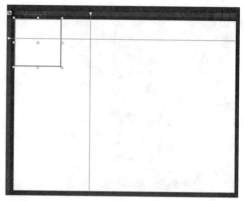

Figure 12.13 A ListBox added to the Artboard.

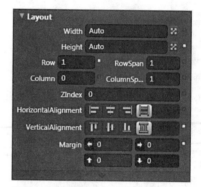

Figure 12.14 Layout properties for the ListBox.

Figure 12.15 Find the Image control in the Asset Library.

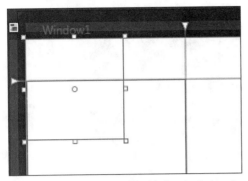

Figure 12.16 The Image control added to the Artboard.

8. After the Image is selected from the Asset Library, double-click the Image icon in the Toolbox to add an Image to the Artboard. **Figure 12.16** shows the default Image control added to the Artboard.

9. To position the Image correctly, change the properties of the Image control to match **Figure 12.17**.

   Figure 12.18 shows the Image properly placed in the Window. You are now ready to add the folder controls to your UI.

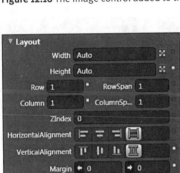

Figure 12.17 Layout properties for the Image control.

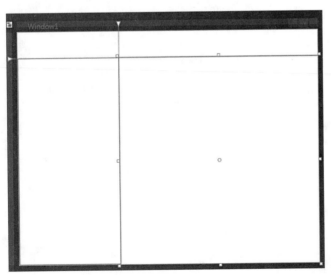

Figure 12.18 The Image control properly placed in the LayoutRoot Grid.

Adding the Folder Controls

After you've built the layout structure for your browser application, you can add controls that enable the user to select an image folder located on the local system.

To create the directory controls:

1. In the Objects and Timeline panel, double-click DockPanel (**Figure 12.19**). The DockPanel on the Artboard is now highlighted with a yellow outline (**Figure 12.20**).

2. Add a Label control to the DockPanel. This Label lets the user know what the TextBox (added in step 4) is for. The Label control is located within the Text tool fly-out menu in the Toolbox (**Figure 12.21**). After selecting the Label control from the fly-out menu, double-click the icon to add it to the Artboard.

3. Edit the Label control text by typing directly into the control on the Artboard. **Figure 12.22** shows the text changed to *Directory*.

Figure 12.19 Double-click DockPanel in the Objects and Timeline panel.

Figure 12.20 The DockPanel on the Artboard is outlined with a yellow border to indicate that it is selected.

Figure 12.21 Choose the Label object from the Toolbox.

Figure 12.22 Edit the label text.

Figure 12.23 Choose the TextBox control from the Toolbox.

Figure 12.24 The TextBox added to the DockPanel.

Figure 12.25 The Button control added to the DockPanel.

4. Add a TextBox control to display the current path to the selected folder. The TextBox control is found in the Toolbox in the Text tool fly-out menu (**Figure 12.23**). After you select the TextBox control from the fly-out menu, double-click its icon to add it to the Artboard (**Figure 12.24**).

5. In the Toolbox, double-click the Button control to add it to the DockPanel (**Figure 12.25**).

To edit the control layout:

1. On the Artboard, ensure that the Button control is selected.

2. In the Layout section of the Properties panel, change the Button control's Dock property to Right (**Figure 12.26**).

3. In the Objects and Timeline panel, switch the stacking order of the TextBox and the Button controls (**Figure 12.27**). Reordering these objects gives the TextBox prominence in the fill space (**Figure 12.28**).

4. Change the label text of the Button control. Select the Button (**Figure 12.29**), and in the Common Properties section of the Properties panel, enter *Change* into the Content property (**Figure 12.30**).

5. In the Layout section of the Properties panel, change the Margins for each of the controls to 5. The controls will now resemble those shown in **Figure 12.31**.

Figure 12.26 Change the Dock property to Right.

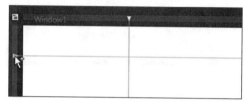

Figure 12.27 Switch the order of the TextBox and the Button.

Figure 12.28 The DockPanel after changing the properties.

Figure 12.29 Select the Button.

Figure 12.30 The Content property in the Common Properties section of the Properties panel.

Figure 12.31 The final appearance of the controls in the DockPanel.

Figure 12.32 The Objects and Timeline panel before setting the Name property.

Figure 12.33 The Name property is found at the top of the Properties panel.

Figure 12.34 The Objects and Timeline panel after setting the Name property for the TextBox and the Button.

To add the Name property:

The Name property is one of the most important of your application's controls. Assigning a Name value to an object enables you to directly access that application object from code. In your application, you need to access both the TextBox and Button controls from the code to add interactivity to the UI.

Figure 12.32 shows the three controls in the Objects and Timeline panel before adding the Name property value. You can find the Name property at the top of the Properties panel (**Figure 12.33**). Assign a Name value of ChangeDirectoryButton to the Button control, and a Name value of DirectoryTextBox to the TextBox control. After you modify these names, the Objects and Timeline panel reflects the change (**Figure 12.34**).

ADDING THE FOLDER CONTROLS

Adding Media to the Application

This WPF application needs to read the content of a folder, display its images, and enable a user to select an image and view a larger version of it. In this section, you import sample images into the application.

To import images:

1. In the Project panel, right-click the project name, ImageViewer, and from the context menu, choose Add New Folder (**Figure 12.35**).

2. Name the new folder *Images* (**Figure 12.36**).

3. Right-click the newly created Images folder, and from the context menu, choose Add Existing Item (**Figure 12.37**).

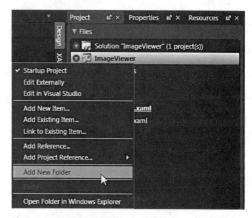

Figure 12.35 Choose Add New Folder from the context menu.

Figure 12.36 Change the name of the folder to *Images*.

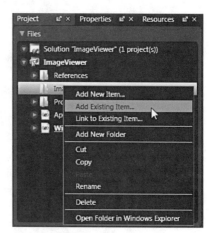

Figure 12.37 Choose Add Existing Item from the context menu.

4. In the Add Existing Item dialog, navigate to one or more images that you want to import to the project and click Open (**Figure 12.38**).

5. The Project panel shows the imported images (**Figure 12.39**).

Figure 12.38 The Add Existing Item dialog.

Figure 12.39 The imported images in the Project panel.

ADDING MEDIA TO THE APPLICATION

Adding Interactivity to the UI

The final step toward making the UI interactive is to add code. **Figure 12.40** shows the running application.

Figure 12.41 shows the necessary code within the window1.xaml.cs file. You can find this C# code file in the zip file of the browser project at www.blendsupport.com/blend-2vqs/files/Ch12_ImageViewer_Project.zip. The code populates the image ListBox with images from the directory specified in the folder TextBox and wires up the main image to the selected image.

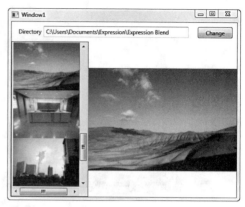

Figure 12.40 The application running.

Note that in the constructor of the class (`public Window1() { }`) you need to register events for the `Loaded` event of the Window, the `SelectionChanged` event for the ImageListBox, and the `Click` event for the ChangeDirectoryButton.

When the `Loaded` event occurs, the application loads images from the default directory of internal images that you imported in the previous section.

When the `SelectionChanged` event occurs, the MainImage changes to match the source of the selected Image.

When the `Click` event occurs, the ImageListBox reloads with images from the supplied directory.

```
 1 using System;
 2 using System.IO;
 3 using System.Windows;
 4 using System.Windows.Controls;
 5 using System.Windows.Media.Imaging;
 6
 7 namespace ImageViewer
 8 {
 9     /// <summary>
10     /// Interaction logic for Window1.xaml
11     /// </summary>
12     public partial class Window1 : Window
13     {
14         public Window1()
15         {
16             this.InitializeComponent();
17
18             //Register events for the Loaded event of the window, ImageListBox item selected
19             //  changed, and the button click for the change directory.
20             this.Loaded += new RoutedEventHandler(Window1_Loaded);
21             this.ImageListBox.SelectionChanged +=
22                     new SelectionChangedEventHandler(ImageListBox_SelectionChanged);
23             this.ChangeDirectoryButton.Click +=
24                     new RoutedEventHandler(ChangeDirectoryButton_Click);
25         }
26
27         /// <summary>
28         /// Fires when the controls has finished loading.
29         /// </summary>
30         void Window1_Loaded(object sender, RoutedEventArgs e)
31         {
32             this.DirectoryTextBox.Text = Environment.CurrentDirectory + "\\Images";
33
34             PopulateImageList();
35         }
36
37         /// <summary>
38         /// Fires when the user clicks the ChangeDirectoryButton.
39         /// </summary>
40         void ChangeDirectoryButton_Click(object sender, RoutedEventArgs e)
41         {
42             PopulateImageList();
43         }
44
45         /// <summary>
46         /// Fires when the user changes an image in the ImageListBox.
47         /// </summary>
48         void ImageListBox_SelectionChanged(object sender, SelectionChangedEventArgs e)
49         {
50             MainImage.Source = (this.ImageListBox.SelectedItem as Image).Source;
51         }
52
53         /// <summary>
54         /// Private function to populate the ImageListBox.
55         /// </summary>
56         private void PopulateImageList()
57         {
58             ImageListBox.Items.Clear();
59
60             DirectoryInfo directory = new DirectoryInfo(this.DirectoryTextBox.Text);
61
62             foreach (FileInfo f in directory.GetFiles("*.jpg"))
63             {
64                 Image image = new Image();
65                 image.Source = new BitmapImage(new Uri(f.FullName));
66                 image.HorizontalAlignment = HorizontalAlignment.Stretch;
67                 image.Height = 100;
68
69                 this.ImageListBox.Items.Add(image);
70             }
71         }
72     }
73 }
```

Figure 12.41 The completed code in Window1.xaml.cs.

ADDING INTERACTIVITY TO THE UI

INDEX

INDEX

INDEX